Scanning, uploading and/or distribution of this book via the Internet, print, audio recordings or any other means without the permission of the Publisher is illegal and will be prosecuted to the fullest extent of the law.

Dancing With Natasha
Copyright©2007 Gregory Causey
With Natasha Yushanov
ISBN 978-1-934446-00-3
Cover Art by Joan Causey

All rights reserved. Except for review purposes, the reproduction of this book in whole or part, electronically or mechanically, constitutes a copyright violation.

Published by
Romance Divine 2007
Find us on the
World Wide Web at
www.romancedivine.com

Greg and Joan Causey receive their Bronze II Dance Certificate.

From Left to Right

Mario Kraszewski: Owner of the Dayton Ohio Arthur Murray Dance Studio

Joan Causey: Dance Student

Greg Causey: Dance Student and Author

Natasha Yushanov: Dance Professional

Terry Irwin: Dance Professional, Choreographer and Judge

Lee Burchett: Dance Professional

Photo by Judy Grigsby

Dedication

*For my dance partner
Joan, all my love!*

Dancing With Natasha

By

Gregory Causey
with
Natasha Yushanov

ACKNOWLEDGEMENTS

Many individuals assisted in bringing *Dancing With Natasha* to life. I'd like to extend my thanks to the following:

The Dayton Arthur Murray Dance Studio staff: Mario Kraszewski, Svetlana Hollenbaugh, Justyna Masajlo, Paula Kirkland, Lee Burchett, Radoslaw "Radek" Rogowski, and Judy Grigsby.

Barbara Haller for her support on this project and for writing the Foreword.

My fellow dance students who participated by lending the time to tell their stories.

Famed Toronto dating coach Christine Akiteng for allowing me to quote from her delightful article: "Do Women Really Relate Sex to Dancing?"

Bob Baemel of Mill Run Photography for the front and back cover photos of Natasha Yushanov and Lee Burchett.

My editor, publisher and friend, thank you Claudia...for all you do and all you are.

Special thanks to my writing collaborator and dance instructress, the irrepressible and most wonderful Natasha.

And to my mother and father, who won the Rumba and Waltz contest at the Fort Huachuca, Arizona Officer's Club.

FOREWORD

by

Barbara Haller

Four-time United States Professional Theatrical Arts Champion.

Dancing with Natasha is a significant and timely work, shedding great light and much levity on the relatively unexplored territory of studying ballroom dancing. In this account a student's firsthand experience is juxtaposed against that of a professional. Beginning student Greg Causey shares, with rare wit, his emotional and physical joys and concerns during the learning process. As you will see, there is far more to the experience than merely taking a few lessons.

In her own inimitable fashion, Greg's capable teacher and collaborator, Natasha, chronicles the sociological aspects of teaching dance. She explores, as well, the range of 'hats' one must wear to be an effective teacher. You can read more about the professionals and students as they share their dance experiences in the cast notes. The benefits they have derived from learning to dance vary widely, from a new lease on life, to childhood dreams, to great cardio.

As one who has made dance her life, I am fully aware of all the physical and emotional benefits of this sport, and can attest to the fact that not only students, but teachers as well, undergo life-altering changes. I am pleased to have been asked to write this foreword, especially as the studio in question is our old 'stomping ground,' where the bulk of our competitive rehearsals and coaching lessons took place. Quite a few of the staff chronicled in this book were personally selected and trained during my tenure at the studio. I am especially proud of the protagonist, Natasha. At the risk of sounding a braggadocio, I did predict she would be a star!

Dancing with Natasha covers a wide range of learning experiences. Some, notably the stage performances, are unique to the school itself. Nonetheless, you who have taken ballroom lessons will identify with Greg and Joan's experiences. You who have taught ballroom dance to adults will appreciate Natasha's insight into the process of turning non-dancers into dancers. And you who have no idea what it is all about will certainly enjoy the read, and may very well find yourselves picking up the phone to call the nearest Arthur Murray's for your own lessons!

Tim and Barbara Haller
*Four-Time United States Professional
Theatrical Arts Champions*

Photos Courtesy of Tim & Barbara Haller

"Admit me Chorus to this history:
Who, prologue-like,
Your humble patience pray,
Gently to hear, kindly to judge,
Our play."

William Shakespeare, Henry V

OVERATURE

Introduction by Greg and Natasha

ACT I

ACT I, Scene 1: I Can't Dance

ACT I, Scene 2: Dance 'Style'

ACT I, Scene 3: "I Am Speaking English?"
Dance Language

ACT I, Scene 4: Teaching Dance

ACT I, Scene 5: "Are You Ready
For Your Lesson?"

INTERLUDE

It's Showtime!
Joan and Greg Dance in Public

ACT II

ACT II, Scene 1: If the Rumba is the
Dance of Seduction...

ACT II, Scene 2: Change Partners

ACT II, Scene 3: Dancing is Sexy

INTERLUDE

An Evening Dancing With the Pros

ACT III

ACT III, Scene 1: I Got the Music in Me…Finally
ACT III, Scene 2: There's a Test!?!
ACT III, Scene 3: The Big Show
ACT III, Scene 4: Denouement

FINALE

We Can Dance!

CURTAIN CALL

What I've Learned:
Lessons on Dance and Life From Natasha

PRINCIPLE CAST

The Professionals

SUPPORTING CAST

The Students

Overature

People ask: "Greg, it must have taken you a long time to write that dancing book. How did you do it?"

My answer: "Slow-slow-quick-quick, slow-slow-quick-quick."

Seriously, the impetus for *Dancing With Natasha* came about on the dance floor as I struggled with fifth position, cross-over breaks, cross-body leads, promenades, and any number of dance moves and disciplines. The struggles, the joy of discovery, the frustrations, and the sense of accomplishment when *it works* more than once made me believe, "There might be a book in all this."

At first it was a joke. As I struggled with the dance moves I'd tell Natasha, "I'm gonna write a book." Eventually I began writing, and when something notable happened on the dance floor, I'd tell her, "That's going in the book!"

What kind of book? That remains to be seen. I think it will be completed long before I become adept at moving my center and mastering the rise and fall of the waltz, despite Natasha's best efforts.

At times I envision this book as a dark, tragic, comedy chronicling the human suffering and despair of one man in Dayton, Ohio. At others, it's a story of triumph over adversity.

I've met a lot of interesting people in the dance world, instructors and students alike. As an author, I have a compulsion to share this experience with others. The people at the dance studio run the gamut of age, gender, occupation, and ethnicity. At local events, you might meet octogenarians along with teenagers, all enjoying ballroom dancing. At the Friday night parties hosted by our studio, I've danced with high school students, grandmothers, women of many nationalities and ages. And we all laughed, danced and enjoyed ourselves, even when we - OK, even when I - danced poorly.

Dancing With Natasha is about dancing, yes, but more than that it's about people and the meaning of dance in their lives. In the following Acts, the reader will journey with my wife and me as we learn ballroom dancing. During the Interludes you will see how we have taken our dance lessons and used them in our everyday lives. You will also get the opportunity to meet real people who dance: salespeople, housewives, university professors, and others who are profiled in the Supporting Cast credits.

I'd also like to introduce you to some of the wonderful dance professionals I've met, and let them share their own personal experiences with you. All of these people are marvelous dancers, and bring unique characteristics and qualities to their teaching, and their interpretation of dance. While the steps and routines in dance are well established, the nuances and variations are as endless as the dancers who perform them. If dance is, as is music, a universal language, then these people are ambassadors *par excellence*! Enjoy their stories in the Principal Cast credits.

As for myself, I've been a musician, playing drums and guitar in a variety of venues over the years: clubs, casuals, weddings, parties, even a recording session or two. Before retiring from government work I spent over thirty years working in a variety of technical and management positions. While living in Maine I wrote and taught a Total Quality Management course at a local college. During the time Joan and I lived in Europe I started writing and presenting my own unique workshops on quality and management. So I've not been a stranger to the arts/music, or in getting up in front of groups and being in a performance or teacher mode. Yet the astute reader may note that this brief bio was woefully lacking in dance experience or accomplishments.

And now, I'd like to introduce my dance instructress and writing collaborator, Natasha. In taking on this work I probably couldn't have asked for anyone better. Natasha is a wonderful dancer, has a great sense of humor and possesses a very prestigious academic and writing resume. She has a Master's Degree in Editing and while pursuing her PhD in Moscow she taught proofreading. In her native Riga, Latvia, she worked at the Riga Evening Daily newspaper as a proofreader.

As with many of us, life takes us in different directions and places. In 1995 Natasha left Riga and moved to Ohio, where she learned English and ballroom dance. You'll learn more about Natasha as she adds her own thoughts throughout the book. Without further ado – ladies and gentlemen, I give you - Natasha.

Gregory Causey

Natasha...

On Writing

When people trust themselves into the hands of the dance instructor, very special type of relationship is created. Perhaps my vocabulary is not rich enough, but the word that comes to mind is...friendship. Let's see – we do meet a few times a week; we are aware of the life events, major and minor; and we share the laughs, sweat and sometimes frustration. We can even get comfortable enough to snap at each other – and forgive one another and hug after that. When we fail – we fail together. When we succeed – we succeed together. On this trip to the destination unknown we are together – yet each of us holds our own end.

When Greg first spoke of writing a book what thrilled me most was the fact that I finally would know what is happening on the other end. The days when I was a student, though vivid in my memory are long gone - I felt I needed this window into the student's perception. Russians say, "The other's soul is a twilight zone," to the outsider that is. I think it takes courage to let an outsider into the hidden passages of one's soul, and I feel grateful for the opportunity to be part of this attempt. Believe me, everything Greg describes was well earned.

There's also something he doesn't describe - and that is, "What does it take to make Natasha follow?" I tried to tell somebody once - they looked at me with great disbelief, but the truth is that for the good part of my life I was completely sure I didn't know how to dance socially. There were enough fingers on one hand to count those rare partners I could dance with - in spite of all this stern Russian ballet training, or shall I say because of it? It took some time to figure out that those few I was able to dance with were good...followers, a quality I could hardly put on my list of accomplishments. From then on I always felt somewhat on a mission, because, believe it or not, about 70% of women who come to the studio don't possess this quality either. And just like the men need to be taught to lead in dance, so the women - these wonderful, strong, confident women - need to be taught to just let go and follow.

From that perspective, working on this book was a very unique experience, because it was completely opposite from typical teacher - student dynamic. Here, like in dance, Greg was in absolute lead and I - I could do nothing but follow. Ladies, let me tell you - following can be fun, if the leader knows what he is doing, which is subject for another chapter.

When it comes to my opinion, or philosophies, as Greg calls it, they weren't formed in one day, and there are many distinguished dance professionals who contributed greatly to the process.

Act I

Scene 1: I Can't Dance!

"Socrates learned to dance when he was seventy because he felt an essential part of himself had been neglected."
Unknown

Having been married to my lovely wife – hereafter known as Joan – for thirty six years, one of the most memorable arguments of our marriage concerned my reluctance to dance. I didn't like to dance, didn't want to dance. I viewed the dance floor as a place of terror, where I would be exposed. To my credit I sometimes tried, venturing onto that wooden wasteland to give it my best effort. Those people observing my various moves, gyrations and contortions might disagree, but for me, I was dancing. I thought. My reticence to engage in what must be a

DNA-embedded, tribal instinct was hard to overcome. Did I suffer from a traumatic, acute dance-performance-anxiety? Yes! There was something inherently frightening about getting up before a group of people and moving my body in that fashion.

And that's odd, because throughout much of my life I've been in a performance mode. Besides my professional musician experience, I've worked as a featured speaker and lecturer presenting workshops on management and quality. But my musical gifts of rhythm and my on-stage, public performance abilities refused to collaborate when it came to dance. To hear Joan's explanation: "Greg's description of himself as a 'dancer' is right on the mark. When we first started dating in the late 60's, he asked me to a dance, and I was excited and in great anticipation. Here I was, going to a dance with a musician, someone I knew understood music. Unfortunately, I soon learned when you took the drum sticks out of his hands, his rhythm, his ability to express the music was gone."

Dance was scary. Dance was intimidating. Dance was something to be avoided. Yet the artist in me, the musician, loved to watch dance: the Nicholas brothers, Gregory Hines, Fred Astaire, the fiery Latin and Salsa dances performed to the complex rhythms that the drummer in me could not ignore. In the small of the night, I savored the movie, *Shall We Dance* and on television, *Dancing With The Stars*. It looked elegant, glamorous and fun. But get on the floor...and do that!?

Time and events, however, conspired to push me forward. What happened? It was a combination of things. Joan's career ascended to a senior executive position, and we started attending more formal functions, balls, dinners, and receptions. Invariably, there was a quartet, an orchestra, a band – and dancing.

Every time I drove by the local Arthur Murray Dance Studio, I looked and wondered...what if...could I? So in January 2006 I found the courage to ask Joan, "Do you want me to go to the Arthur Murray studio and see about dance lessons?"

Naturally, she said, "Yes."

So we began our dance sojourn, not knowing where it would lead. Our lives were destined to become a flurry of dance activities: private lessons, semi-private lessons, coaching lessons with visiting professionals, group lessons, Friday night practice parties at the studio, evenings out with the professionals, and certification tests. We were about to embark on a life changing event.

Gregory Causey

𝒩*atasha...*

On Beginners

January of 2006 was a busy time at the studio – new students were flooding in, gift certificates in hands, and the teachers had to spin fast to get everyone in the schedule. That is when Greg and Joan walked in with their dream to dance at the high echelon party with the appropriate style. You know how sometimes you meet people – and they take you into the equation right away? Well, that wasn't the case with these two. It took them a while to warm up and let me, if not in, then at least close enough so the lessons would become more than strictly business. It was fine with me, because I could see in them the driving force for any endeavor – and that is determination. No matter what it takes they were – and still are – determined to be graceful and elegant on the dance floor – so we will go until they feel graceful and elegant to their highest standards.

I can relate to that – and that is why we clicked.

Dancing With Natasha

Since then we had our share of fun and hard work mixed together to make steady progression that is sometimes hard to feel for the students, but is never missed by watchful eye of the professional. I don't know what is the mark other teachers look for in their student's progress, to me it is that day when they surprise me with some beautiful move of their own, something that doesn't look like they have taken lessons, but rather were born that way.

"Who taught you this?" I'd ask in amazement.

"You did," they would laugh.

That is when I know that if I vanished tomorrow they will keep dancing...and - sh-h-h-h, it's a big secret, but Greg and Joan passed this point.

ACT I

Scene 2: Dance 'Style'

"The truest expression of a people is in its dance and in its music. Bodies never lie."
Agnes de Mille

The very word "ballroom dancing" derives from the Latin word of "ballare," meaning "to dance." While the tradition of dance may be as old as man, much of what we do in today's ballroom dancing lies heavily on the earlier foundations of Arthur Murray, Fred Astaire and Ginger Rogers, and Vernon and Irene Castle. And if you're talking about elegant and classy dancing, that's not bad company to keep.

As with any art form there are various styles. In ballroom dancing the accepted styles are American and International. Joan and I are learning the American Style, but there are more similarities than differences between the two.

Dancing With Natasha

American style is divided into two categories: smooth and rhythm. American Smooth contains the Waltz, Tango, Fox Trot and Viennese Waltz. American Rhythm consists of the Cha-Cha, Rumba, East Coast Swing, Bolero and Mambo.

These categories are not meant to denigrate, by their exclusion, such wonderful dances as the Samba, Country Two-Step, Hustle, Merengue, Salsa, Polka, or any number of other dances that are popular regionally or world–wide. Indeed, in learning ballroom dance I've found that the various dances share many similarities in their moves.

During my brief research of the history of dance, I noticed a few writers bemoaning the death of couple's dancing and big band music, laying the fault directly at the feet of Rock and Roll. As one of the generation who grew up on Rock and Roll I don't want to be burdened with that guilt: the death of ballroom dancing.

I'm not a sociologist or anthropologist, but it seems that all forms of art and expression evolve, adapt, and reflect their time and technology. During those waning years of ballroom dance, people were still dancing. I'll admit that rock music and the dances it spawned tended to keep the dancers apart. But at the same time, and I can vouch for this from my perch on the drum riser, people still danced together. I saw country dancers holding each other, twisting and turning, watched people hustle and disco, and witnessed the mambo / salsa craze. And now...classic ballroom dancing is again gaining in popularity.

Art changes, grows and evolves. Artistic expression builds on the traditions of its past Masters. Ballroom dancers of the 1920's and 30's might view what passes today for ballroom dancing as *not quite proper*. But that's OK, because dance is an art form, an art that reflects our culture and values. And if I wait long enough that Nehru jacket from 1968 will be back in style.

Gregory Causey

Natasha...

On Dance Styles

Speaking of the Nehru jacket and the revolving of fashion: In 1910 among other popular Ragtime dances with very colorful names like Crab Step, Kangaroo Dip and Turkey Trot, there was a dance named Chicken Scratch. Seventy years later this dance resurfaced in Arthur Murray International, Inc. syllabus as the variation for Cha-Cha. Don't know how close to the real chicken scratching they got in 1910, but the Cha-Cha variation I had to learn was certainly suitable for the name: rock-step-cha-cha-cha, scratch-scratch-cha-cha-cha.

According to the chart of dance crazes provided by Arthur Murray International Inc., right after Chicken Scratch there was Foxtrot in 1912, Tango with Rudolf Valentino in 1921, Charleston in 1926, Lindy Hop in 1927, Rumba in 1930, Swing in 1934, Merengue in 1941, Mambo in 1944, Cha-Cha in 1952, Bossa Nova in 1962, Hustle in 1975, Disco in 1977, Lambada in 1989, then Argentine

Tango, Salsa (considered by some to be "street Mambo"), and back to Lindy Hop in the 90s. Hold on to your jacket, Gregory!

Today ballroom is hot, couples dancing prevails, any style, any dance, even theatrical Paso Doble – as long as it takes two to dance it. After tearing away from each other to gain more space for self-expression we are back to seeking closeness. It is very much about resurrecting feelings of togetherness that people seem to be after in dancing.

There's a cliché about dancing being the best marriage insurance policy in which one could ever invest. One of our long time students whose wife, as he swears, was transformed solely by dancing from modest house-maker into dangerously sexy vamp-woman, jokes that if the marriage can survive taking dance lessons, it will survive anything – hence the insurance.

Quick Step or Paso Doble – the Arthur Murray system is flexible enough to teach whatever dance is in demand. When the new dance catches public attention the "Ambassadors" from Arthur Murray travel to the countries of origin to absorb the style, to learn it first hand – and teach the eager.

Whatever the style - at the beginning there was a dance. They claim that quite a few patterns in contemporary ballroom dancing were born out of mistakes made in existing steps and gracefully presented as part of the dance. Others were derived from authentic dances that were raised by the tide of ever-searching fashion – like Rumba or Mambo. Cha-Cha, supposedly, was born because Mambo was too fast for general public to keep up with, so they slowed down the music, used a syncopation to spice it up – and voila! Cha-Cha it became.

So whatever the style, at the beginning there was a dance. It felt good. It felt uplifting, for those who knew how. Those who knew how were moving freely, they were expressing themselves and impressing others. Those who didn't dance were standing around full of envy. Then somebody who knew how and felt for those who didn't, came up with an idea – let's see how it is done and teach others.

I believe that the style of dancing varies from person to person, and you'd look and feel your best moving to the music in the most natural manner – natural for you, for your body. Our job as instructors is to see what is your natural manner and give you the guidelines on how to enhance what you already have – which is essentially the permission to be yourself, your best self, the daring and free one, the self of your dreams.

There are many techniques that we can teach you – and all of them would be only tools that allow you to create your own masterpiece of dance. To the best of my knowledge all you are going to do while dancing is to use the force of gravity that is affecting natural dynamics of two bodies connected through the common center and applying the pressure against the unmovable floor and movable each other. It's pure physics and some anatomy – which do exist and work whether we are aware of them or not. Learning how to dance is learning the relation between the cause and effect, action and reaction. You want a nicely sized gliding step? Flex your knees and go with the heel. For smaller steps use the toe lead. Put the book down and try right now to make a big step tip toeing. Does it work? See! Edward Simon, United States American Ballroom Champion, World Showdance and US Theatrical finalist who we are so fortunate to have visit our studio as coach and choreographer, has a saying that, "If something feels uncomfortable while dancing, you are probably doing it wrong." Encouraging philosophy, isn't it?

So, whatever the style, at the beginning…there was a dance.

Act I

Scene 3: I Am Speaking English?

Dance Language

"Dance is the hidden language of the soul."
Martha Graham

Natasha, our dance instructress, where to begin? The fates must have conspired to put Joan and me together with Natasha.

The title of this chapter, "I Am Speaking English?" is not a condemnation of Natasha's language skills. She often asks the question as she demonstrates a dance technique, and turns to see me with that glazed, deer-in-the-headlights look. "I am speaking English?" she asks. Natasha speaks very good English. The problem is that I have been slow in learning the language of dance, and especially slow in translating that language into the corresponding movement of my various appendages. But I'll admit it; Natasha's accent does add a wonderful, international flair to our dance experience.

All disciplines, the arts, technology, business have their own language, their own terminology, phraseology and acronyms that often make that discipline mysterious to outsiders. As a musician it was quite natural for me to tell other musicians at a jam session that, "This tune is a Be-Bop blues in B-flat, with a quick change, trade fours on the last chorus, and tag the ending." And we'd kick off the song and play, no problem. Business people do the same with their, "The CEO wants the EOM report by COB and cc the CIO on the IT extracts."

My wife is a senior finance executive, an accounting and business professional. I can't tell you the number of times I have accompanied her to business dinners, sitting there dumbfounded and bewildered as finance speak streaked across the table: "GAFS won't interface with CDS, you still need to account for expenditures, receivables and in-transits to get CFO compliant; and you definitely don't want an ADA violation." I'd knowingly nod my head and ask the waitress for more bread.

So I wasn't surprised to find that dance had a language of its own. I've learned to not be overly intimidated by such terms as second-position, fifth-position, twinkle, cross-body lead, chasse', and more.

I still sometimes confuse the Sweetheart and the Peek-a-Boo moves in the Cha-Cha. Joan also struggles with terminology, trying to connect the name of the dance to the steps needed to execute the movement. Often Natasha puts on a piece of music while Joan leans forward and whispers, "What's this one?"

"A Rumba."

"That's the...uh...the box thing...right?"

"Yea, the box thing, like the Waltz."

There are other words that come to mind when I consider the *language* of dance. One of those words is egalitarianism: "Maintaining, relating to, or based on a belief that all people are, in principle, equal and should enjoy equal social, political, and economic rights and opportunities (Encarta Dictionary)."

Dance is a great leveler between the sexes. It's an activity where the man and woman are on equal footing. Despite political correctness and equal opportunity, one seldom sees men and women engaged as equal partners / competitors on a football field, baseball diamond, or delivery room. In most cases genetic differences prevail against total equality.

But dance...dance is different, it's a true partnership, each partner reacting to the other, complementing the other, moving with and against each other, in a state of egalitarian equality. On the dance floor men and women co-exist as equals, although women do have to do it all backwards, and in high heels.

Another word that describes dance is civility. There's an old-world elegance, formality and manners associated with dance, social graces lacking in many of our modern, day-to-day encounters. Ballroom dance requires etiquette; the man approaches the woman, asking if she would like to dance. If the woman accepts, the man extends a hand, and the woman steps forward into dance position. When the dance is over both parties thank each other and the man escorts the woman from the floor.

As a beginner I've witnessed this ritual and taken part in it. I've nervously approached a woman, cautiously extending a hand and asking, "Would you like to dance?" or, "May I please have this dance?"

To their great credit, and my fragile ego, the women at the Friday night dance parties graciously accept my dance invitations. Afterwards I always thank them, sometimes offering a slight bow, a homage to the culture of Europe.

In an electronic, voice-mail, e-mail, fast-food age, this genteel, almost courtly ritual is a welcome throw-back to a time when social manners and decorum were more observed.

Gregory Causey

𝒩atasha...

On Dance Language

OK, I have to admit – sometimes whatever it is I am speaking is not exactly English, and I know that. Reminds me of the encounter I once had with the lady who's husband was born in Cuba. He had quite a life story, full of adversities, and his wife was very proud and protective of him. The man spoke impeccable English, and liked things to be done well, if done at all. Dancing was tittering on the edge. Once, after all three of us broke into well earned sweat on the lesson, the lady suddenly turned to me and said with one of those meant-to-be sweet face expressions, "You do realize, of course, that you will never get rid of your accent?"

Caught me off guard, for I really wasn't trying to get rid of my accent. My chiropractor, for example, finds it intriguing, and thinks it would be very helpful in getting bigger tips as waitress. See, we never know what might come in handy.

Dancing With Natasha

Dance business hosts a lot of professionals with foreign background. Our studio is not an exception. There were times when two-thirds of the staff spoke with various accents. Often I thought it was appropriate to warn new students, though jokingly, that it usually takes about forty five minutes to get through my accent, and if not – we will find them someone who speaks better English. Interesting observation was made by one of my colleagues from Europe. "Isn't it peculiar," he said, "that in some matters your native tongue is not your first language anymore?"

True! Everything I know about ballroom dancing for instance, with the exception, perhaps, of the names of the dances, I have learned on this very floor, in English. If someone would ask me to teach it in Russian or Latvian I would get lost on the first box step.

It is not the dance terminology though, that makes my mouth dry from talking, and when it does, there are always 'Curiously Strong' mints – the daily diet of dance instructors. It would go dry in attempts to translate the terminology into the language the student can relate to. There are, hidden in the back rooms, massive volumes of dance manuals, that meticulously describe every twick of muscles the partners make gracefully commencing to an inverted left spiral while moving side and slightly forward on the last quarter of the beat number one. Now translate it to someone who is still despairing over the decision which foot to move since there are two of them…what English would you use?

Of course, there are certain trends. Speaking of equality of genders, it is known that men and women don't use, nor do they respond equally to the same language. Let's say, women grasp the concept of the inside-outside turn much easier than most men, to whom the same turn described as clockwise-counterclockwise makes significantly more sense. If you ever plan to teach dance, here's the suggestion – never use words Right and Left, whether it comes to position of the head, feet, arms, and especially turns. You'll have a long argument about whose left it is we are turning to – and as result both partners will end up pulling in opposite directions.

When the words fail – which happens to me occasionally because I am still working on expanding my vocabulary – I use tools and demonstrations. The only thing that I remember from my very first lesson taught is that in desperate search for words I asked the man not to be like the tree in the wind – and showed exactly what I meant. Surprisingly he understood and straightened up. To this day I don't know if this imagery was the reason they stayed around – but then again, my merciful memory didn't keep any other evidence of that lesson; and that is good, I suppose.

What comes to using tools, it's a 'live and learn' process. One of the most popular tools in our studio is the stick – and I remember the time when the broom was still attached to this stick, so dancing with the broom was not a figure of speech. Besides the broom the students are also dancing with trays, making circles around tables, stepping up and down the sidewalk, pushing the walls, opening and closing doors, throwing imaginary balls – can't give them real ones because of the mirrors, and suffering in what I call 'harness' – the only professional device we happen to have that is specifically designed to help the man keep his frame intact. Did I forget anything? Oh yes – one couple presented me once with the toy whip – which was their loving way to call me a 'task master,' but I have learned since how to be convincing without it, and it rests in my locker along with the riding crop – that too.

Frank Reagan, a legend in ballroom dancing and show-business, taught me a good lesson. We were having a coaching session on Waltz, and to my surprise Frank put my student up to the ballet bar. "The man needs something for his balance while trying to feel his body," he insisted. The student was an engineer, and listening to him and Frank talking I felt refreshing need for a dictionary, Webster technical or something. I was standing there in awe, and not so much out of reverence for Frank's vocabulary, but because after using all these twenty dollar words he took the student to the bar so he could FEEL the action. Why didn't I think of that?

But that's what these coaching sessions are about – enlightening equally the student and the teacher. In the daily routines, however, the teacher relies on domestic recourses. You know Physics? Shoot! Some sports? Pull it out! Seen the ocean? Played games? Been to the doctors? Whatever common experience can be found – as long as both parties can relate to it. It's an every day trial and error process that helps the teacher to create a vast collection of ready-to-use explanations – depending on who is listening.

I remember how excited I was when the term "centrifugal force" firmly attached in my mind to the concept learned in Russian. Eager and enthusiastic I used it on the very next lesson. "It's easy," I said, "to make it flow nicely, just use the centrifugal force."

The gentleman looked at me bewildered, scratched his forehead and said with uncertainty, "Uh, Natasha, I am a meat and potatoes kind of guy."

ACT I

Scene 4: Teaching Dance

"I don't want people who want to dance; I want people who have to dance."
George Balanchine

In the movie Pure Country, George Strait talks to his drummer about going to the fair and seeing the dancing chickens. It turned out that the chickens were dancing on a piece of cloth that sat over a hot plate, so when the man turned on the hot plate under the chicken's feet...the chickens danced. Sometimes I feel like that dancing chicken, not because my feet are on fire, but that I'm randomly moving and responding to external stimuli. It's the job of the professional dance instructor to teach their chickens to really dance and not simply flop about on the floor.

Dancing With Natasha

Teaching dance can't be an easy gig. One must have mastery of the many dances. The dance instructor must know both the ladies and men's patterns. A dance instructor requires the technical skills to judge the student's talent and abilities, breaking the dance into those various sequences that the student can comprehend. The instructor needs keen powers of observation to be able to detect the student's mistakes, correct inadequacies, and provide solutions to problems. The technical skills required to teach dance seem formidable.

In addition to the purely technical requirements an instructor has to be a people person, perhaps the toughest component of all. The dance instructor needs to be a guide, coach, facilitator, salesperson, motivator and cheerleader. Some of these skills can be taught - I know - I've conducted workshops on these topics. But for the successful dance instructors, this comes naturally. They love dance, and they love working with people.

The professional dance instructor must help many of their students overcome one of the greatest fears that people possess: public performance anxiety. To this end the good dance instructors need to be something of a therapist. They must help people overcome their fears, whether those are fears of performance anxiety, or fears of the intimacy associated with dancing.

All of this represents a tremendous challenge to the dance instructor. Not only does the professional dance instructor have to teach technical skills, they often have to effect behavioral changes rooted in very real fears.

Dancing is supposed to be fun. And it is...when you get over the trepidation of dancing. Granted, not everyone has a fear of dancing. I envy those who can hit the floor and let it go. Watching other beginning couples on the dance floor, I've noticed other nervous eyes and hesitant steps, so I know that I'm not alone in my original dance reticence. There's an actual clinical term for the fear of dancing called Chorophobia. Although I believe that my particular issue towards learning dance was caused by Ataxiophobia: the fear of muscular incoordination.

The best dance instructors feel that same joy of accomplishment that their students feel when they get it right. Often a cry of delight is heard in the studio as a dance instructor exults in their student's success. By the same token I must give credit to instructors who motivate themselves for teaching the same things, over and over to a continuous parade of new students.

For dance instructor Mario Kraszewski, it's always "Good morning!" his standard greeting, even at night. Since Mario believes that morning is the best part of the day (he has obviously NOT seen Joan on an early Monday morning when she has a day of business meetings scheduled) he feels that it should always be a good morning for us. There is no question he is up-beat; the man has personality and exuberance to spare. He is a born entertainer and performer, and he makes dancing fun. To me, he represents the quintessential dance instructor.

One of Joan's most memorable lessons was one of the first we did with Mario. As we arrived for our lesson we were told that Natasha was not available due to an emergency and that Mario would be conducting our lesson that night. Leading us onto the floor he began working on Swing. He led Joan around in several fancy turns, things we'd never done, and she followed effortlessly. For Joan the evening was a high point early in our lesson program. She was given an idea of what was possible for her in the realm of dance, and she felt that if she and I could achieve half that level of expertise the effort would be worthwhile. Mario's skill, humor and personable style made a big impact that evening.

The dance instructor: artist, technician, therapist, teacher, psychologist, trainer, salesperson and coach. Tough gig!

Gregory Causey

Natasha...

On Being A Dance Instructor

I have to admit, the suggestion to talk about the difficulties of being dance instructor threw me into the surge of deep gratitude towards Gregory. Then the dilemma arose – does he want me to be honest or diplomatic?

When people come to the studio they expect to be in the happy place. That's what they say – verbatim, "Ah, it's such a happy place, everyone is always smiling."

I knew a man who, after he learned that dance instructors don't smile 24/7 was greatly – no, not disillusioned – hurt and disappointed. I guess he thought the professionals were born dancing and smiling – and that's how they leave this world too. Which is pretty close to reality, of course, but not always. I remember the words of wisdom I got as a trainee from Mario, who was one of my instructors. We were speaking Russian and he said: $%#@(*&^%-@!!^&*$*. The part that can be officially translated sounded like, "People think it's an easy job! Oh, yeah!?! It's harder than to work in construction, only we get to put on nice clothes." I had to agree, because my feet were killing me – and that was just the beginning.

Let's mention up front though, that the moment instructors start looking at stumbling points as being "difficulties" of teaching dance, they are dead on the dance floor. Believe me, I tested it myself – bad idea. Whatever makes us sometimes stumble are not difficulties, but rather challenges that make this job what it is – a quest that lasts as long as we are willing to stay on it. And just like for the students, the dance quest starts once they walk in the door for the first time, so it does for the specialist – the teacher who greets them at the door, the one who says, "Hello, my name is...I am going to be your instructor for tonight...welcome to Arthur Murray...let me show you around..." What did I say so far? Nothing much – just a greeting, yet while those words are being said people have already decided if they are going to listen to me any further or not. Which will become obvious on the very next question, "What made you decide to come to the studio?" If they like the teacher they will go at length explaining what and why, when and where. If they don't like the teacher...well, there are still twenty seven minutes to help them to change their mind. So they better be fun, these twenty seven minutes, they better be easy, they better be all about them – the students – and them only, and besides we do need to teach them some dancing. Because once the first lesson is over, they either feel like they have done the right thing coming in the door, or else – there's no other chance.

Challenging? Yes – but also fascinating. In thirty flying minutes, if we have done it right, these people will start to believe that dancing can be fun not only for the lucky others, but for them, too. They will start to believe that maybe, just maybe, their hypothetical love for dance can be mutual. Somewhere on the first lesson there will be this quiet click, and a secret door will open for more…no matter how many times I have heard this "click," it's still magic.

If you remember the first elation of falling in love, you must also remember that there came a day when to maintain that elation you needed to see where it was taking you - and perhaps make some conscious effort towards that direction. Same with dancing. The excitement over the fact that: We can move! To the music! And not embarrass ourselves! can fade fairly quickly. Still, there are people for whom such quick dance romance is fulfilling enough. For those who seek a long lasting relationship with dance we have the appropriate tools to make it work: goals, tests, competitions, shows, and above all – yes, our own love for dancing.

I heard once wonderful words said about the dance

business, "Luckily for all of us, the amateurs and professionals alike, in dancing everyone is always a student." Luckily, because tapping into the unknown keeps the excitement alive, and as long as the teacher is capable of excitement – the students are in good hands.

Potential job seekers, under "position" often write "Dance Instructor." What a misleading combination of words! Teaching dance is not a job, and dance instructor is not a position – it's admittedly a style of life. Those who don't understand that are out the door quickly. Those who do understand have the hardest time letting go even if life is calling to move on.

It takes a lot of diverse abilities to become a good dance instructor, but the most beloved ones I had the honor to work with through the years first had a big heart and the rest of it was added. When a group of teachers and students visited Camp Samaritan, the Ohio summer camp for cancer survivors, we danced and we talked to people. Warmed up by our dancing, and dancing with us, they opened up sharing their thoughts and feelings. One man unwrapped his philosophy for us – the philosophy he acquired through dealing with his illness. "When I talk to someone," he said, "there's nothing and nobody more important to me at the moment than this person."

I thought, "Hey, isn't that what we are doing every day – and call it teaching dance?"

Act I

Scene 5: "Are You Ready For Your Lesson?"

"They whip up curds, hoping it might turn into cream."
Johann Wolfgang Von Goethe
Maxim no. 73

The dance lesson: where the music, the moves and the mood come together. It's that intimate, one-on-one, or one-on-two time when the professional dance instructor creates their magic, bringing the gift of dance to the... OK, so maybe it's not always that magical. Sometimes it can be grueling.

The dance instructor conducting the lesson reminds me of Goethe's quote above. Sometimes that's how I feel, not particularly curd-like, but rather that I'm being churned in the blender of dance until my skills on the floor achieve the smooth, rich, silkiness of fine cream.

Occasionally however, I feel more like lumpy cottage cheese. But it's the dance lesson where the instructor's skill and expertise meet the student's dreams and desires that makes the magic.

I've had 'lessons' throughout my life: guitar lessons, martial arts lessons and flying lessons, so I felt familiar with the pedagogy of lessons and teaching. But neither Joan, nor I, were prepared for the myriad of lesson types that awaited us on our dance journey.

There are semi-private lessons, wherein a group of students work on one dance: basic Merengue, Cha-Cha variations, or advanced Rumba technique.

At the Friday night practice parties we have a group lesson half-way through the evening. One of the instructors teaches a specific dance move combination for the group.

We enjoy coaching lessons with visiting professionals Gabriela Young, Pat Traymore and Terry Irwin. Joan and I dance a bit and Natasha and the visiting pro evaluates our dance and then hone-in and work on specific technical aspects.

To really work a technique we utilize the full-potential lesson. In a full-potential, Joan takes a lesson with Lee, while I work on the identical moves with Natasha. When those individual lessons are finished, Natasha takes Joan and I, and has us work on the moves together.

But the staple of our program, the bulk of our learning, is done via the private lesson. The private lesson goes something like this: Joan and I arrive at the dance studio and change into our dance shoes, which provides a ritualistic transition between the stresses of the day into a dance frame of mind. This seemingly innocuous change of footwear redefines our whole mode of bi-pedal locomotion. No longer will we walk, stroll, or amble; now we dance.

Depending on the number of students on the floor we may go out and practice. If students are getting a lesson in the Fox Trot we will work on our Fox Trot moves. Perhaps we'll try to execute a technique we'd learned from a previous lesson. Sometimes it works and we're elated, but often it doesn't work as well as we would like.

We practice at home, pushing the kitchen table out of the way, the wood floors providing much the same feel as the studio. Occasionally we successfully remember the moves; often we don't. If we are unsure about a particular dance step we don't practice it. As beginning students, Barbara Haller told us that while practice makes perfect, there's also such a thing as "practice makes permanent." It's best not to develop bad dance habits Natasha will have to correct.

At some point Natasha, our lesson binder in hand, appears and leads us to a small table flanking the studio floor. Opening the binder she scans the contents and declares, "We start with Tango." Joan and I take the floor as Natasha starts the music. I hold Joan in my frame, trying to remember the various nuances in posture and hand position, little details that take the dance to the next performance level.

Usually I do a few basic steps to get into the dance, to get the rhythm going and settle in. Then I'll work in some of the moves of that particular dance. Oftentimes I get locked in those basic steps while I fervently try to collect my thoughts and plan my next move. Unfailingly, Joan gets bored, and issues a command, "Do something."

Natasha may call out moves; this is called 'being the brain,' where she is thinking for me. This relieves me of that incredibly complex process of holding the woman, moving my body in time to the music, thinking of what to do next and giving the woman the necessary physical clues for her to execute her moves. For the uninitiated, this process is called…dancing.

The lesson contains much starting and stopping, as Natasha makes adjustments to our technique, coaching us on proper foot placement, perhaps working on the rise and fall, where our heads should be, our body alignment and so on. Seldom does anything new come easily. I've found that breaking down the movements into smaller pieces and then working through each step slowly yields the best results. Often I must do it again, and again, and again in a drill-type fashion so that my body begins to react in the proper sequence with the proper timing. It's no different than playing scales on a piano or saxophone, building up dexterity and muscle memory until the necessary unconscious fluidity is achieved. But those things occur over time; rarely does anything come together on the first try.

I've been made to dance with a stick, holding it horizontally, cradled in the bend of my elbows. This teaching aid reminds me to maintain my frame as I move over the dance floor. To develop my balance I've moved across the floor, one foot passing the other, like walking on a railroad tie, moving straight ahead, keeping within the narrow confines defined by lines on the parquet floor.

There's much to remember. On the Tango I must keep low ("Sit on your pony," commands Natasha), support the woman with my hand in her back, and *not* look at her except for that brief moment on the Flare Promenade.

Natasha often uses two fingers on her right hand to make little 'bunny ears' to keep my head focused in the correct direction: "Watch the bunny, look at the bunny." It sounds stupid...but it works. Joan has also picked up the 'bunny ear' habit.

We never know what the lesson will entail: learning new steps, or polishing and refining moves we've previously learned. Each lesson usually focuses on more than one dance, sometimes even three. Natasha senses when we get to a point of diminishing returns on a particular move, and she switches to something new, coming back to the problem move at a later time when our minds and feet are fresh.

At the end of the lesson Natasha will ask us what we've learned and we dutifully recant the sacred mantras recently given us. She furiously scribbles in our binder, making the various notations that indicate our ability with certain dance steps.

Some days and some lessons are better than others, but anyone learning a new skill encounters peaks and valleys in the attempt. For my part I know that when we go to the Friday night dance parties Joan and I can actually dance, and put to use the tools and techniques that the instructors painstakingly teach us. So the lessons are working. We're learning to dance.

Gregory Causey

On The Dance Lesson

There was a time when preparation for the lesson was taking me longer than teaching one. Being only a couple of steps ahead of the students makes anxiety a regular overtone of life, and it takes a long time to get rid of nightmares in slow-quick-quick rhythm. But just like students first learn the basic components, then the patterns made from the components, and only then get the freedom of using the components in a creative way, so the teacher, after meticulously following all the rules at all times learns to be creative and flexible. Not only do people learn differently, different people want to be taught differently. Some just want to have fun. They don't care how much they learn, they don't care how much they will retain by the next lesson as long as they are having a good time moving with the music they are happy. Then there are complete opposites, who make notes, practice any spare moment, do their homework and get disarrayed beyond repair if instead of the scheduled lesson on the Waltz they are offered to work on Swing. Between these two extremes there's vast variety of attitudes and ambitions, and each of them would require a different planning lesson. No matter what I plan, however, the actual lesson is going to be just like dance, where the leader which is me, the teacher, would offer the direction, and the follower, which would be the student or couple, would follow the direction offered; to the best of their ability, that is.

I plan to work on Tango. We haven't touched Tango for a while, and now finally the more socially practical dances seem to be in steady shape, so Tango it is. But when the lesson starts, the music machine is playing Fox Trot, and really there's nothing wrong with doing Fox Trot as a warm-up dance is there? After all, it is the easiest one to follow, and to lead.

Fine, "Let's warm up with Fox Trot," I say. They start dancing and make a mistake. Not a big deal, but a couple of patterns later, the same mistake again. We spent a few lessons working on this particular detail, yet here they are bravely dancing like they never heard a word about it before. OK, this is not in the lesson plan, but if I don't correct it now, by the time we get back to Fox Trot according to curriculum the mistake they make will turn into bad habit. So we slow down and fix the mistake. When finally it is all corrected and learned anew I look at the clock...we still have half a lesson. The tricky part, however, is that the man's mind is so conditioned to Fox Trot by now - switching to Tango, which is another 'walking' dance, would cause great confusion, frustration and precious time wasted. Lesson plan abandoned, we take Cha-Cha next. So much for Tango, maybe next time.

Life happens. We may have planned to work on the rise and fall in Waltz, but they came in the door and informed me that they had a bad day at work, and besides last night till dark they were carrying the mulch and everything is so sore, could we please do something fun and easy? Like Merengue...please? Or we planned a lesson for the stage routine, and in the meanwhile two wedding couples, each with their own song, got scheduled at the same time, so now we don't have enough floor and not much hope to get to the music. After all, who wouldn't wish for the newlyweds to do the best they can possibly muster in the week and a half they allowed us to spend on their first dance? I look at my student..."Let's do some technique," I say. "Let's work on Cuban motion."

INTERLUDE

It's Showtime!

Joan and Greg Dance in Public

Part 1. "Do you want to dance?"

June 9, 2006, our coming out party was the realization of months of dance lessons. Joan and I attended her annual Financial Management Ball. The usual program for these events is cocktails, dinner, and a guest speaker, followed by dancing. Joan and I may, or may not, step onto the floor, clutch each other, and move slowly to the music. Before Arthur Murray came into our lives we called it dancing, that one obligatory dance before we escaped to the parking lot.

This night was to be different. Tonight we would dance, in front of other people. A small trio played a medley of songs and invited folks to dance to the music. As the musicians began to play Joan looked at me and asked, "What would we dance to that?"

My mind furiously envisioned the rock-step, triple-step, triple- step pattern and I replied, "Swing."

Looking resplendent in her black, beaded evening wear she asked, "Do you want to dance?"

I was feeling confident in my black tuxedo, red cummerbund and matching tie; confident that she wouldn't move because she wouldn't want us to be the only couple on the floor.

"Yes, sure, I'm ready when you are" I replied.

Neither of us moved. The trio played on; they were good.

She looked at me, "So do you want to dance?"

I nodded, "Yea, sure, if you do."

The dance-fear G-forces restraining me to my chair were incredible. To keep from blacking out I flexed my thighs like fighter pilots do. No one moved.

"OK," she said, "Let's do it." She rose from her chair, and somehow I escorted her to the dance floor.

The portable parquet floor that previously looked small now loomed before me, a veritable limitless expanse of foreboding hardwood. We stood alone on the floor, facing each other, holding hands. Waiting for the 4 count, the last beat of the measure, I subtly pushed her back to start the rock step on one.

We were dancing, a real dance, to live music, in a ballroom, in front of other people. I tried to relax, smile, and not count out loud, "Rock-step, triple-step, triple-step." Together we did our moves, rotated clockwise, and we were dancing the Swing.

"Do something," said Joan.

My mind raced to think of all the Swing patterns and moves that I knew. *OK, I can do an under-arm turn.* So we did that, a waist roll, and walks and points.

When the band finished their number we went back to our table. We'd danced the first dance of the evening, alone on the dance floor, in front of everyone else. The trio's third song had a Latin flavor.

I extended a hand to Joan, "Rumba?" We rose and went to the dance floor a second time. And for the second time we were alone on the floor. We did our Rumba box pattern, open and crossover breaks, Cuban walks, and underarm turns. I thought we were much showier on the Rumba than on the Swing.

We danced more that evening, doing a variety of Fox Trot, Rumba, Cha-Cha and Swing steps. I danced with two other ladies, and Joan danced with another gentleman. We were among the last to leave that evening.

The experience left me in a bit of a dance shock.

Dancing With Natasha

We'd gone from essentially never dancing, or doing the obligatory one-slow-dance grope, to being the first ones on the floor, and dancing more than anyone else.

In retrospect, the original mission of our dance lessons had been accomplished. We were dancing at the formal functions Joan is required to attend.

Joan enjoyed herself as never before and I conquered much of my fear. I'm still a bit intimidated on the dance floor, but now we'll do it for fun!

Part 2. "Step away from the slot machine...and dance."

July 4, 2006 found Joan and I at the Venetian Resort-Hotel-Casino. With its great rooms, wonderful restaurants, shops and gambling it's our usual haunt when we go to Las Vegas. I'm not much on gambling, that Joan's pleasure. Instead I like to relax in one of the lounges, enjoy a Cognac, listen to the band, and watch people. Oh, and there is a dance floor.

The question is how to tear Joan away from the Casino. It's not easy. The first night I reposed, alone, with my Cognac, in the lounge. The second night I laid in wait.

Finally Joan entered and I escorted her to our table. We listened to the band and waited for a suitable song. When they launched into a Swing beat we hit the floor.

We were dancing in a club, in a big name hotel, in Las Vegas!

Part 3. "We've got the fever."

July 29, 2006, we attended another formal affair. A colleague of Joan's invited us to a Quinceanera, a traditional Puerto Rican coming out party for a fifteen year-old girl; marking her transition into womanhood. It was an event steeped in culture and ritual, very memorable. Afterwards there was dancing.

After the dinner we danced the rest of the night doing lots of Swing as well as Cha-Cha, Rumba, and a Waltz or two. Some of Joan's colleagues from her previous company were quite impressed with her newly-found dancing skills.

We took our dancing shoes, and changed into them before the dancing started. That's how far we were succumbing to this dance fever.

Nowadays we go out, we dance, we have fun. I would have never imagined spending most Friday nights dancing, but that's what we do now. The first thing we look for on formal invitations is a reference to dance. Dancing has, and will continue to be, a significant part of our social life.

Gregory Causey

Natasha...

On Putting the Skills to Use

Couple of years ago the most frequently given reason for people to start taking dance lessons sounded just like that: "We got tired to sit out at the party when everyone else is dancing." Rarely would someone walk in the door and announce upfront that they want to compete – and win, too. *Dancing with the Stars* changed this tendency dramatically. The idea that someone can learn the showmanship of dance in fairly short period of time made a big breakthrough in people's minds. Oh, they still want to get ready for their own or their children's weddings, get socially more equipped for the cruises, mingle with the style at the professional gatherings, but the look they want to acquire in dancing is way up high now – everyone wants to look like *Dancing with the Stars.*

It's exciting – and challenging at the same time. Exciting because people come in the door with their eyes already lit, their expectations soaring. It's challenging for the same reason – the eyes are lit, the expectations are soaring, and here we are – starting with the basics.

Long time ago I heard the story of the man who walked in the door on December 28th to learn how to dance for the New Year's Eve party. Three months later, being in a good mood after particularly successful lesson, he admitted to his teacher: "That's how I thought I'd be able to dance at the party I was going to."

Thanks to the "dance movies" and *Dancing with the Stars* we are back to showtime. More so – those aficionados of the popular show who pay attention not just to the performance part have more realistic idea of consistency that is needed to learn how to dance well.

Of course we still have wedding couples coming in the door a week prior to the event – and we do our best to help them. But, overall the fact that muscle memory takes many repetitions to develop is not such a big surprise to the general public any more. We learned at the last teacher's conference in Chicago that there are programs a' la *Dancing with the Stars* offered at some studios – where students are taking between five to eight lessons every day for a week or two, and then show off at specially designed studio event. Now that is what I call intensity!

When I first read this chapter, I thought – what can I possibly know about how our students feel about dancing publicly for the first time? Maybe only that time when my friend and I were pushing the cart at the grocery store, and this crazy tune came up on the radio, so the next thing I knew he was twirling me around, cart and groceries forgotten, in wild Jitter Bug. Or perhaps when I went to the wedding and soon enough the entire wedding party, ladies and gentlemen alike, were standing in line to dance with me, because I was, "The only one who knows what you are doing."

But no, that wouldn't count, because I wasn't a student at the time. I'll tell you one of my favorite stories. The man and wife were saving money for the honeymoon. It was somewhat belated honeymoon, actually – in the meanwhile they raised four children, built the church and invented something totally awesome in the cable industry – so it was almost like renewing vows honeymoon, and they were very much looking forward to it. Finally the trip was booked – it was to be St. Maartin, and it was to be in a month. If before we were working on what is called social biggies – Fox Trot, Waltz, Rumba, Cha-Cha, and Swing, to fit the demand of the exotic trip we switched to Salsa and Merengue – all this beach-appropriate stuff. I couldn't wait for them to return and tell me all about it. As the story goes, the honeymoon, even though long waited for, was magical! Incredible! Marvelous! Terrific! Unbelievable! They fell in love with the island and had the time of their life. They didn't dance much though, except for one night, when they were strolling barefoot along the beach and suddenly heard a slow Waltz being played at one of the on-the-shore restaurants. So...they looked at each other...dropped their shoes...and Waltzed - under the stars.

Act II

Scene 1: If the Rumba is the Dance of Seduction...

"If I could tell you what it meant, there would be no point in dancing it."
Martha Graham

If we look back to the early roots of civilization, tribal dancers wanted to invoke the rain or harvest God, danced to ensure a good hunt, prepare for war, or seduce a mate. It was all about telling a story, creating a mood.

Whenever we can, Joan and I attend the Friday night parties at the studio. These opportunities give us a chance to put into practice all those moves we have learned. Mid-way through the evening one of the instructors conducts a group lesson. Men and women each take a side of the floor and one of the pros teaches a few steps from a selected dance so that we can perform them singly, then take a partner and try them again. Next we'll change partners and do it again. By the end of the group lesson I've usually danced with each of the ladies at least twice.

The first few times we did this I found it very unnerving. On one of these evenings, as we changed partners I was paired with Natasha. The dance we were learning that night was the Tango, and Natasha fixed me with a penetrating gaze saying, "If the Rumba is the dance of seduction, the Tango is the final act." Then she struck this absolutely killer dance pose, waiting for me to take her in my arms. Panic and fear were my first two emotional responses. Despite my initial fear I learned a valuable lesson...each dance means something.

One thing I am learning from Natasha, one thing I have not yet mastered, is that dance is theatre. When you dance you are telling a story. You are an actor performing a part.

Natasha excels at this; she is a dance-drama queen. It must be her *Slavic* roots, that heritage of ballet, symphony and literature: The *Bolshoi*, *Tolstoy*, *Tchaikovsky*, *Borodin*, and *Rimsky - Korsakov*. When Natasha strikes a pose it is art worthy of the Hermitage.

She attempts to pass this on to Joan and me. But what passes for the seductive Tango of the Pampas Gauchos when performed by Natasha ends up as a fumbling comic act for us. I understand where she is going, what she wants us to do, but comprehension and execution are, for now, mutually exclusive concepts.

I now see dance in a way I'd never envisioned. Sometimes, as I take Joan into a dance hold, in my best Antonio Banderas voice I tell her, "You are my woman," at which point she breaks into hysterical laughter. The moment is ruined, and poor Natasha can only stand there, waiting for us to compose ourselves. In spite of the hard work and extensive effort required to learn ballroom dance, we wouldn't continue if we didn't enjoy it. Silliness cuts the tension that can occur when the learning curve is steep.

The tilt of the head, the seductive lengthening of an arm, each move conveys a message: 'Go away, come here, I'm ignoring you, I want you.' Ballroom dances tell a story, enacting a scenario of pursuit and seduction.

As frightening as it is to get out on the floor and dance it gets worse when one is told to 'vamp it up.' It's the old performance anxiety thing again. Yet it's exactly that kind of theatrical approach that turns the standard routine dance moves into a true piece of performance art.

It's probably no different than those method acting coaches who have their students imitate a piece of bacon frying or a tree in the wind. It's all about getting in touch with the part, the role that you will play. If one can bring that to their dance, it raises the level of the performance considerably.

Of course knowing this and writing about it is a lot different than making it happen on the dance floor. As I said, "I get it," and I'm slowly learning how to do it. I'm committed to bringing more performance to my dance. As Hamlet said, "The play's the thing."

Gregory Causey

𝒩*atasha...*

On Dancing the Story

You don't have to take my word for it, but they say the Rumba, and most Latin dances with their basic rhythm quick-quick-slow (or slow-quick-quick), are originally derived from the African ritual dance of the rooster and the hen. Which reminds me of this old joke: "What does the hen think when being chased by the rooster? She thinks, 'I hope I am not running too fast.' The rooster thinks, 'Even if she gets away, I still get my exercise.'"

Here's Tango in the nutshell: the man is after the woman, the woman is playing hard to get, he insists – she refuses, he gets angry – she gets stubborn, and if she still gets away – he still gets his exercise does he not?

Or Rumba, the man is after the woman, the woman looks into his eyes and thinks: "I wonder if I move my hips a bit more where will he lead me?"

Or Bolero, the man is after the woman and the woman goes: "Oh, but I shouldn't - but I want to - but I can't."

I am not sure about the Waltz and Polka, but my

guess would be, and I pray to be forgiven by historians of dance, that the man was still after the woman and was winning her heart by spinning her around and keeping her warm, because it's much colder in Europe than in Africa.

Whatever the climate, as long as people are dancing together, the basic story behind it is the same; it's the nuances of the character that can make the dance party into the elaborate development of the relationship. He takes her for a walk in Fox Trot. He spins her head around in Waltz. He melts her in Rumba. He makes her laugh and let down her guard in Swing. He deepens the groove in quick and hot Salsa. He attacks in Tango. He eases the grip in silly Merengue. He makes her dizzy in Hustle. Once she is totally dizzy and confused he begs for her love in Bolero. And it is in Samba when she shows him what she is capable of...if he can still move after Samba, "Shall we go for another walk?" in the Fox Trot.

If you don't like the story make your own...but do tell the story, because the story is the soul of dance. Somehow, somewhere it has to be about the rooster and the hen.

Otherwise there's always a treadmill.

Act II

Scene 2: *Change Partners*

"Dancers are the athletes of God."
Albert Einstein

I am dancing with other women! For the last fifty-plus years I've not danced with anyone other than Joan, notwithstanding the dancing done with Natasha during our lessons. So to be experiencing a new discipline, dance, with many different woman can be challenging. It can be intimidating to touch another woman with your own spouse or significant other in attendance. Intellectually, I know that it's simply a class, or a party, and we are all doing it, all changing partners and dancing with each other. Still, I experience moments of trepidation.

While researching the history of ballroom dancing I

came across the fact that the Waltz had its origins in The Volta, a piece of music from 1500's France. In order to execute the turn, the partners had to be so close that many found the dance to be immoral, and Louis XIII banned it from his court.

I also discovered that after his release from Landsberg prison for his ill-fated 1923 Beer Hall Putsch, Hitler's friend Helene Hanfstaengl tried to talk him into learning to Waltz. She felt this would improve his social graces. Her husband told Hitler that great statesmen and generals such as Washington, Napoleon, and Frederick the Great all liked to dance. Hitler's reply was: "A stupid waste of time and these Viennese Waltzes are too effeminate for a man to dance." Would things have turned out differently if one of the worst tyrants in history had learned to waltz and discovered a more cultured side of his personality?

Men, in our relations with women, have enough performance anxiety without the additional impetus of having to lead them through dance moves, making them look beautiful and glamorous. Coupled with the performance anxiety that goes along with dancing with someone else is the: *What if I'm not good enough?*

I've watched the male dance instructors on the floor, the professionals, guys who know how to get it done. In their competent hands, they make their partners look graceful, beautiful and seductive. That can be frightening to the beginner. Our partner stands before us, waiting for us, the male, the one who leads, to transform her into a beautiful gliding swan or a frenzied Latin seductress.

Even with all of this angst I feel ballroom dancing is for everyone, couples and singles alike. It provides a form of intimate, social contact. When you hold your partner you establish a personal, human connection. While cheeky banter is not forbidden, you must be aware of each other, and communicate non-verbally. The man must give his partner space, support her in his frame, and provide her the lead so she knows where to go, what to do, and looks absolutely fabulous while doing it. That's a lot to do with your spouse or significant other, but is even harder with a stranger. However, if you can do that, think of the connection you have made with that other individual: two distinct individuals, in sync, in real time, and moving as one.

Will dance succumb to the lure of technology, to become another high-tech, digitized, instant, virtual, on-line entertainment medium devoid of human intervention? I hope not. My fear would be walking into the dance studio to be greeted by some kind of high-tech kiosk. It might go something like this:

"Hello. Welcome to high-tech virtual dance studios. Your patronage is important to us. This transaction may be monitored for quality purposes. All virtual dance instructors are currently busy. If you know the code of your virtual dance instructor you may press the 4 digit code now. If you would like to Cha-Cha, please press 1. If you would like to Waltz, please press 2. If you would like to Rumba, please press 3. If you would like to Fox Trot, please press 4. To dance the Swing, please press 5. To dance the Tango, please press 6. For all other dances, or to speak to a virtual operator, please stand by. To hear this list again, please press star. Hello. Welcome to high-tech virtual dance studios. Your patronage is important to us........"

That's not what dance should be about and I hope it never gets to that point. If you agree with me please press 1. If you disagree please press 2.

Natasha...

On Dancing With Partners

It was in my first year of teaching, in the time when Arthur Murray studios were still using syllabus created in 80's. One of the variations in Tango was called medio corte with the leg crawl. I thought personally it was really cool variation, where in corte position a lady would slide her bent leg up and down the man's outstretched leg. It looked very dramatic, and I remember the only question I had to more experienced dancers was how to do the crawl without revealing the length of the man's socks in the process.

Once, this variation was taught in the group class on Friday night. While the entire group was working on the medio corte everything was going smooth, but the very moment the teacher announced the crawling part, the lady who that particular night was at the party without her husband, suddenly left the floor. I went to her thinking she is not feeling well, and was met by furious, "Should have known not to come by myself!"

Dancing With Natasha

As both of us took a deep breath, she explained in so many words that she finds this variation indecent, would never dance it with anyone but her husband, and is done with the group class for tonight. In the meantime the rest of the students were cheerfully passing on and receiving the crawl, clapping and making jokes. Nobody thought much of it, just dancing. Altogether, even if, at first, some very new students refused to change partners in the beginners group, by second class they felt comfortable enough to let go and experience the variety of leading and following styles of the different partners.

Again, everyone is different. For some the social aspect of dancing would be that they can dance, to any music, anywhere, with anybody, dance and keep the pleasant conversation going. For another it would be to go and mingle with other fellow dancers having the club of common interests, but not necessarily changing partners in the process. Yet for some it would be that they can get on the floor in front of everyone, have the time of their life, and be the celebrities among the non-dancers.

The studio phone is ringing starting early morning. Traditionally it is thought that people go dancing in the evening, after the day's work, but some of those early calls make me wonder. Every now and then someone will call and ask if they have to have a partner to take lessons in the studio. These are the people for whom the social aspect of dancing is the main aspect, at least initially.

Gregory Causey

They come in the door because they are tired of being lonely, and if they stick around long enough to make it through their first party you can almost guarantee they are going to stay with us for a while. There's something about it, the idea that every Friday we dress up and dance to our heart's content, no matter what's the weather. For some we literally become like a substitute family, all of us, the students and the teachers together. This is something I know about first hand.

When I started working as a teacher I had an empty house, I didn't have anywhere to go, nor did I have much of an idea where do people go when they don't want to be alone; and just about everyone I knew in town was either teaching or taking lessons at Arthur Murray. To be quite honest, I didn't even know where to start counting my blessings, because it's hard to describe the full life I had - and still have - by merely coming to work and doing my "normal" job. I got to go out every day, spiff up and all. I was interacting with wonderful, interesting people who were teaching me as much as I was teaching them. I got to dance every day; this was, and still is, just like heaven. When I look back over this time it gives me a pretty good idea what it must feel like to some of our students. It makes one feel...happy!

Act II

Scene 3: Dancing is Sexy

*"Dancing is a perpendicular expression
of a horizontal desire."*
George Bernard Shaw

Dancing is sexy. Or at least it can be, if it's done right. Admittedly, my ballroom dancing data pool population is based mostly on the past year's experiences. But in my opinion women are sexy when they dance. That combination of evocative music and sensual body movement makes dancing a natural erotic act. By the same token, a hot Jive Swing can embody a lot of fun and humor, as well as sexual energy. Of course there are degrees and gradations of this phenomenon exhibited by each of the participants.

Painters, musicians, writers, even comedians observe the world around them and reflect that in their art. We comment and expound on our observations of the human condition. And if the human condition is wearing a slinky beaded evening gown with high-heeled dancing pumps and is exquisitely coiffed and made up; that might merit just a bit more observation by the artist. But we want to make sure we get our observations right.

There may be something tribal, perhaps eons old, some rhythmic component of our DNA helix that strikes that resonant dance chord within us. There's a rhythm to the universe, to our environment; the beating of our heart, the chirping of a cricket, the croaking of a bullfrog reinforce a natural rhythmic and harmonic convergence that we eventually express as dance. And it's not just us, only humans. Zoologists describe the dance-like mating rituals of many animal species. Dance provides one the chance to strut, tempt, taunt, preen, and show off their plumage. As a non-verbal communication medium dance may be at the top of the heap.

For man, dance has long been a unifying communal effort. Whether cultures and customs had male-only, female-only or mixed dances, dance brought people together. Wedding dances, balls and feasts provide a rich pageant of mankind's need to express elation.

It was often at these events where a woman, attired in her dance finery, would catch the eye of a young warrior or nobleman. At various points in our history these balls were the primary source for the meeting and mixing of the sexes.

As men and women meet at dances today, they still often costume themselves, wanting to look their best on the dance floor. One should never be surprised to see the ubiquitous fashion staple, the little black dress, at one of the Friday night parties. Eye-catching jewelry, perhaps sequins or lace, something soft and flowing may be found on the ladies. I've found off-the-rack suits and sport coats to be a dancing hindrance for men, so fashionable shirts and well cut slacks provide the usual gentleman's wardrobe.

Dressed in such finery, ensconced within an accepting community of their peers, the dancers release themselves to the music of the night. As the lights twinkle and splash from the mirrored ball and the bass thumps from the speakers, men and women, accountants and teachers by day, become seductive, sexy dancers by night. Feet glide, hips rotate and torsos undulate as the dancers enjoy the freedom provided by the setting.

I believe freedom is critical. Dance gives us the opportunity to adopt another persona, even if only for a few brief moments. It's during the dance that the woman can be the sexy vamp, the man the dashing cavalier. During those three minutes of evocative music that stirs the passions of the soul, the man leads and the woman submits and follows. Or, in some instances, if you ask

Joan, the female lures the male into submission and allows him to assume that leading is in his best interest.

I'm glad to say that I'm not the only one to subscribe to this 'dancing is sexy' theory or to actually put it in writing. Toronto-based dating coach Christine Akiteng, in her wonderful article "Do Women Really Relate Sex to Dancing?" says that women do..."Relate sex to dancing."

"We believe many women judge a man's sex potential by his dance moves." Christine, her friends and colleagues think that they can, "...tell what kind of a lover a man would be by the way he danced."

This may not be what the male population wants to hear. I can imagine what must be going on at the Friday night dance socials at the studio. I can picture Gloria and Jean in the corner.

Gloria: "Did you see Greg's Fox Trot?"

Jean: "Yes...poor Joan."

In unison they look at each other and nod: "Poor Joan."

There is, I suppose, some good news in all of this. Christine says that, "...when a woman has tasted the pleasure of dancing in the arms of a good dancer, it is next to impossible to settle for anything less..." That's good news...IF you're the good dancer, which is one reason I'm taking dance lessons.

Christine further states, "Dances like the tango, salsa and ball-room dancing are some of the most passionate and graceful dances around...(the)...music touches women in a profound and unique way - it stirs their soulfulness. Dance...unlocks the playful and sensuous side of her personality."

One night when we were watching a torrid dance routine by two of the professionals on *Dancing with the Stars*, Joan turned to me and remarked, "Dance is like sex without the intercourse, it's about the closest you can get to real intimacy without getting naked." My immediate thought was, *uh...do you want to dance?*

What Joan likes is that when we dance, my attention is focused on her. She says dancing is, "Fun, I enjoy it, I've never laughed so much."

And maybe a little sexy, too?

Gregory Causey

Natasha...

On Dance is Sexy

There was an old movie about the leader of the union movement, where the heroine says to the man she likes, "Kiss me, because if the kiss is good then everything else will be good as well." It is left to our imagination what "everything else" she is referring to, however the message is quite clear; everything else that would ask for intimacy. Similar to Christine Akiteng, I used to have a theory that if people can find the way to one another through the dancing, everything else that would ask for intimacy between them, "Will be good as well." Let's say up front that intimacy doesn't necessarily mean bluntly sex, however it's not uncommon for the empty-nesters, for instance, to discover that dancing turned out to be one of the best aphrodisiacs they ever found. But beyond this…when people can talk with each other on the heart level isn't it one of the most intimate things one can experience? More so when people don't have to talk, when they understand each other without words. Even the most self-assured, self sufficient, independent ones, aren't we all looking for the chance to be heard and understood, just as we are, for the permission to be ourselves? Hence dancing; for dancing opens these doors for us.

Is dancing sexy? Oh, it surely can be, as sexy as you are willing to make it, for you are the ones mixing the ingredients. All we do is teach you what the ingredients are, and how the chemistry works; which can be quite tricky sometimes. How do you show what you want them to do in order to look, or, what is more important, to feel sexy - and remain politically correct? I remember one of the old time teachers saying, "The man who learns to dance is not interested in dancing with his sister." Well, technically he has been proven wrong because we have seen brothers and sisters learning how to dance together, and doing a good job at it too. But ultimately, yes, the man who is learning how to dance, unless he really has this calling for self-expression through dancing, is nine times out of ten looking for the opportunity to impress a partner. To teach him how to do it takes a lot of dancing around, literally and figuratively speaking. Dancing is very strong medicine, derived from nature too, but unless you are aware of all the side effects, "Don't operate heavy machinery while being under the influence."

Interlude

An Evening Dancing With the Pros

When we signed up for additional dance lessons we received a special present, a Starlite excursion. This was an evening out, with the professional staff, a limo ride to a local dance club, and a night of dancing with our instructors. It sounded fun, perhaps even a bit decadent and glamorous. It turned out to be all of that and more.

The limo ride was exquisite, an elegant, stretch limo, upholstered with sumptuous leather, finished with wood paneling, containing a very well-stocked bar and twinkling lights in the ceiling. On the way to the club we enjoyed chilled Champagne and Chambourd.

Dancing With Natasha

Our destination was a popular upscale restaurant and club outside of Cincinnati. The club's subdued lighting, rich wood, carpets and drapes added warmth and elegance to the atmosphere. On a raised stage a local group churned out dance tunes, a collection of old and new hits. We'd come in style, dressed in our finest dance wear, to a classy club with some great live music; our dance expectations were high.

Yet Joan and I shared a mix of anticipation and anxiety; there was that edge of fear. Not only were we out dancing in public, we would be dancing with the pros. The comfort factor that Joan and I had when dancing with each other was gone. If memory serves me well, as the events of that evening still swirl in foggy vapors within my cranial neuro-receptors, I may have danced with Joan twice, certainly not more than three times.

The plan for a Starlite excursion calls for the students to spend the entire evening dancing with the instructors. This is high-intensity, total-immersion dancing. The participants for this evening included the professionals: Svetlana, Natasha, Mario and Lee, and the students: Linda, Joe, Joan and I.

We'd barely arrived at the club when Svetlana took my hand and led me to the dance floor. Thus began a night of relentless dancing, abated only by short breaks for appetizers and Cognac. Svetlana and Natasha never allowed me a moment's rest, while Lee and Mario did the same to Joan. And not knowing how to do a particular dance, say the Samba or the Merengue, turned out to be *no* excuse for not taking the floor.

The band started a song and Svetlana grabbed my hand, leading me to the floor.

"What's this one?" I asked.

"Merengue, you know Merengue?"

"Uh...no...I..."

Svetlana never broke stride, leading me directly to the floor, grabbing both my hands, and teaching me the basic footwork. Once we'd fallen into a regular rhythmic routine she started with the moves, twisting and turning both of us until I started to suffer a kind of dance floor spatial disorientation. Like a pilot in a white-out, I lost sight of the horizon, or in this case the bar.

She did the same thing with the Samba, yet another dance with which my lack of familiarity did not prevent me from learning on-the-spot. This didn't have the complicated twists and turns of the Merengue, but it was a much faster dance.

Dance protocol insists that the man lead, and the woman follows. A man who possesses these leading skills can take a woman through many movements and make her look beautiful on the dance floor. This requirement to effectively lead is a reason it takes longer for men to develop into competitive dancers than it does for women.

Dancing With Natasha

More than once, Joan and I have struggled on a move, when, to my surprise, Joan executes it quite well with Lee. I'm the problem; I'm not leading.

Couples can grow comfortable with each other's dance styles, learn to act and react to the other's moves. The 'change partners' group lesson at the Friday night parties and the Starlite excursions remove that familiarity. In order to dance well with others, men must have those leading skills. For those of us who've not yet developed our leading skills, female dance instructors have a way of 'back leading' us through a movement, getting the man to the right place at the right time in the right position. Much as a skilled male partner can assist the female, they can make the male look more accomplished. Svetlana did this many times during the evening.

After the initial shock I began to see it as both a fun and educational experience. It was fun to put ourselves through all those twists and turns, to enjoy the occasional raised eyebrow and approving nod from an onlooker. Even though I didn't remember the moves, couldn't repeat them on my own, it was educational because it showed me how the dance 'could' be done and how much fun yet awaited me as my dance skills increased.

When we arrived at the club Lee and Joan took the floor immediately. For Joan, the rest of the evening was, in her words, "A blur." She danced predominantly with

Lee, and because he was one of our instructors, his style was familiar to her. But Lee, as Joan was to learn, is a true performer. He led her through moves she had never attempted, talking to her continually as they danced. At first she was unnerved by the continual banter, as she was trying to concentrate on his lead and make sure she followed correctly. But she soon realized that he was simply trying to get her to relax and enjoy the dance. As Joan told me, every mistake she made, Lee covered and they just kept dancing. After a brief repose to catch her breath, Mario whisked her to the floor.

Joan had only danced with Mario once before, so she wasn't sure what to expect. She found Mario was, "...a passionate dancer," and with him she, "...felt every move, every beat. Mario dances from the top of his head to the tip of his toes. His love for the art is evident in every step."

During the evening Joan and I saw each other mostly during turns on the dance floor. She was kept in a constant whirl by Lee and Mario, but she was happy, having fun. Until now it never occurred to me that my fear of dance had so long denied her this simple pleasure. Feeling that regret, I want desperately to make it up to her.

Throughout the evening we danced Samba, Swing, Hustle, Cha-Cha, Mambo, and Merengue. I danced a Rumba with Natasha and we worked on the banquera opening with the sexy, second position break afterwards. I executed it…sort of, and Natasha responded with, "OK, now do it sexy."

It's no stretch to say that we danced the night away, or at least from the time we entered until we left the club. Never at the Friday night dance parties, nor at the functions Joan and I attend, had we danced so much. If one of the goals of a Starlite excursion is to provide an up-scale, total immersion, real-life dance experience for the student then it was a resounding success. Yes, we were tired and our feet hurt. But, Joan found it to be "exciting and exhilarating," and wanted to know, "…when we could do it again" because we'd had so much fun. We'd seen what social dancing could be; the bar had been raised. Our original goal to dance at Joan's professional functions had earlier been realized; however dance is a journey, not a destination. And we'd just been shown one of the stops along the way.

Gregory Causey

Natasha...

On Starlites

When we were first presented with the idea of Starlites – the upscale outing for the students with dancing one-on-one – it seemed splendid, but somewhat out of reach. None of us was taking limo rides on a regular basis, so it was something to absorb, to get used to. But – it's easy to get used to something nice quickly.

I am not sure who in Arthur Murray Inc. invented Starlites, but I believe they are quite popular for two reasons. First – they are worry free. The only thing the students have to do is get themselves to and from the studio, we take care of the rest. Second – it's somewhat elitist club within the club, where many new ideas are discussed, where the teacher and the student get the chance to talk more than they would on the lesson or at the party, where the night club style of dancing is not only appropriate, but promoted.

Starlites are very intense – true. One night is

considered the equivalent of three regular lessons, because technically we stop only for hors d' oeuvres, or if the student calls for a break. The students love it because they get undivided attention and the training that is delivered inconspicuously – limo doesn't count. This is the only function that studio has where the student gets to dance with the professionals socially – all night long. The teachers love it because it's a nice chance to dance the way they would rather, outside the studio too – limo doesn't count. And yes – we try to make sure that whether the student knows the dance played or not, he or she is still on the floor – we will cover the mistakes, that's what we are there for.

I believe that the Starlite members are to be shown as the best dancers they could possibly look, and if they don't know something – hey hold on me tight, I'll take you through. I used to have a student-partner for the Starlites, who when he didn't know what he was doing strategically would put me between the gazing population of the club and himself. I found it funny, but it worked. I have also noticed that students who would stick to syllabus at any other studio event experience the burst of creativity dancing at the Starlites. Whether this sudden confidence is the result of dancing with a professional who will save them if something doesn't quite work out the way it was intended, or perhaps Champagne with Chambourd is to blame – does not matter. What matters is that they are trying their wings in becoming spontaneous dancers – and that is exciting to witness and to be part of.

All and all, Starlite is not just late evening at the fancy bar – it's a workshop for the stars in making, someone who'd steal the floor, someone people would talk about later: "Remember them guys in the limo? Boy, do they know how to dance!"

Act III

Scene 1: I Got the Music in Me...Finally

"And those who were seen dancing were thought to be insane by those who could not hear the music."
Friedrich Wilhelm Nietzsche

Especially since I consider myself a musician, this one hurts because dancing has given me a new appreciation of music. Even though I've spent years as a drummer, playing on stages for weddings, dances, parties, and club appearances, it wasn't until now that I've actually felt the music as a dance medium. Of course I always heard the beat, kept the time. I can play in 3/4, 6/8, a swing, shuffle, 4/4, I can play in 5/4, 7/4, and Latin grooves. But I never related it to what the dancers were doing because I didn't dance. I didn't know what my arms, legs and feet were supposed to be doing in time to the music.

At one of the Friday night studio parties Mario announced that the next dance would be a Rumba, and the song that came over the music system was *Behind Blue Eyes* by the *Who*. My mind blurred to find a connection between a rock song and a seductive Latin dance. As many times as I've heard and played that song, it never occurred to me that it had a Rumba rhythm. But as Joan and I danced, I heard, and felt, the music in an entirely different way. And yes, we danced a Rumba.

Now when I hear a piece of music I think about what dances could be performed to that particular piece. I even try to visualize the steps in my mind. Of course, in my mental imaging I always dance absolutely fabulous; Natasha would be proud.

In the past, music for me was a player's medium, more intellectual and technical, what phrases could I play over a chord change, how could I play that blues turnaround, how fast could I play this guitar lick? I seldom related the music, the beat, the rhythm to what a dancer did: the slow-slow-quick-quick, or the slow-quick-quick moves of the dancer's feet. Today, when I sit around the house playing my guitar I find myself concentrating on getting a good rhythmic feel, anticipating what my feet, as a dancer, should be doing.

It's no coincidence that, in the past, many musical

aggregations were known as dance bands. People danced for entertainment long before television, video games, and other high-tech amusements became available. Musicians had a better feel for playing dance music. I remember, in my younger days, watching American Bandstand, and enjoying how the teens would rate a record (those round, black, vinyl things that contained music), and commenting that it was "easy to dance to."

My Uncle, David Causey, tells a story that illustrates this well. He was a very successful singer and guitarist in the Decatur, Illinois area. Many years ago he and some talented musicians formed a new group. The band leader explained that a band could be very talented; the individual musicians could be the best in the business, but the band could not succeed if they were not playing music that people could dance to. The leader of the group arranged for all the members to take basic dance lessons so they were well acquainted with what the dancers needed from the musicians. Dancing was the reason people were coming to the clubs and events. If a particular band wasn't playing music the people could dance to the people would look for a band, and a venue, that did. David's band enjoyed many years of success and were always in demand because they understood what their customers, the dancers, wanted and they provided it.

As a drummer I used to play with the time, do those

tricky, showy, technical things that might impress other musicians, but mean nothing to the dancers on the floor. It's a case of knowing your audience; there's a time to display those virtuoso, musical skills, and there's a time to give the dancers a good beat. Dancing has made that point to me in a manner that no amount of lecture or discourse ever had.

Gregory Causey

Natasha...

On Dancing to the Music

Now, promise not to laugh, but here is the story: a long time ago a couple was just starting lessons in their Bronze program, having the most fun with Jitterbug of all dances. And that's what we were working on when the woman noticed another couple gracefully gliding around the floor.

"What is it they are dancing?" she asked me as she hungrily watched the dancers passing their feet in patterns I did not know.

I looked. I listened. The music was slow, and that was the only thing I could say about it. So I guessed, "That's probably Waltz." After the lesson I went to the teacher to ask what his students were dancing.

"We were working on the Fox Trot," he said.

That day I learned two things. First, Fox Trot is indeed a slow dance. Second, Fox Trot and Waltz looked very much alike to me.

You've promised not to laugh.

When we explain what the Friday night parties are good for, among other things we say, "We announce the dances for you, so it trains your ear to recognize what dance comes with what beat." That's exactly what happened with me, one day the Fox Trot/Waltz dilemma wasn't dilemma any longer, and simple count to four helped to sort the rest of the dances too. It doesn't happen that easily for everybody, but then again how many of the students have the blessing in disguise of listening to the same songs every day, over and over and over and OVER again? Especially if each of the songs is clearly labeled, this is Rumba, this is Mambo, that's Merengue. It's fool proof!

Sometimes people come in the door and warn the teacher upfront, "I have two left feet and no rhythm." Aside from the joke that everyone has rhythm as long as they have heart beat, let's clarify. It's not the rhythm that one may lack, but more the concept of rhythm. I have seen one of the most brilliant coaching sessions on rhythm given by Robert Long, National Dance Director of Arthur Murray International, Inc. Bob starts from the idea that the woman is supposed to follow the rhythm the man is dancing, whether it coincides with the beat she hears in the music or not, thus his training is geared towards the man. He explains that the rhythm is kept by the bass. Then Bob places the man under the speaker and asks for a Fox Trot. They would listen together for the bass.

"This heavy low boom-boom-boom underneath all the sounds, do you hear it?"

The man nods with uncertainty.

"OK then," encourages Bob, "Try to nod your head or tap your foot with it."

Once the man hears, separates all of the sounds and finds this magical bass, he'd tap or nod unmistakably.

"Great," soars Bob, "Now let's find out how many beats there are between the big booms."

And that's how he leads the man from Fox Trot: "Boom - ts, Boom – ts," to Waltz: "Boom – ts-ts, Boom – ts-ts," to Rumba: "Boom – ts - chicka-chicka, Boom – ts - chicka-chicka," counting with him to two, three, four.

Magically all the confusion dissipates, the man is beaming, his partner, if there is such, looks at Bob adoringly, and I know that from now on if they get off the beat, it's because the man wasn't listening, not because he didn't hear. Even today, when we take our students to the club, and they ask nervously, "What do we dance to this?" guess what I am counting? "Boom - ts, Boom – ts."

Counting is good; counting is helpful when you are learning. I know many people who develop a habit of counting to themselves while dancing to make sure they stay with the beat. There was a couple who I thought had a lovely interaction while dancing, the man always whispering to his wife something that was apparently very funny because she would always giggle in response. *How wonderful*, I thought, until one day the woman just stopped in the middle of the dance and burst into laughter. Both her husband and I stood there waiting until she could talk.

"This is impossible," she said, wiping her tears. "Can you imagine, he looks in my eyes and goes 'rock step-cha-cha-cha, rock step-cha-cha-cha.'"

I suggested he change the words from "rock step-cha-cha-cha," to "You are beau-ti-ful," with the same rhythm. This time they both laughed and the situation was resolved. So yes, counting is helpful. Even if I am not counting out loud, my "counting machine" is always on, ready to kick in if the student is losing the beat.

However, counting is not enough. The music has slow downs and speed ups, it has crashes and silent notes, and if we are talking about expressing the music through our motions and emotions we better pay attention to these nuances.

The best vehicle to learn this is a choreographed dance, or the showcase routine. In our studio we do theatrical performances, we dance the routines on the real stage with props and lights, selling real tickets and entertaining a real audience.

All of the above puts real pressure on the dancers to be very expressive, so even the people in the last row get the story we are telling through our dance. Now we are talking about the essence of dancing, where counting for rhythm is well passed. There is an inside joke that we are the only studio where people are dancing to the words and crashes of the song, not so much to the beat. That is not true; we do dance to the beat. However, both of our beloved choreographers, Terry Irwin, who is the Director of the show, and Ed Simon are extremely musical. Sometimes the tape of the choreography will sound like this, "So, on this za-ta-ta I want you to pause, and then there are two crashes, one after the other, the small and the big. I want you to go down on the small, and up on the big and *no counting*." What this does, however, it teaches the dancer to be aware of the dynamics in music and to match them with dance expressions. Learning the show routine versus just learning how to dance according to the syllabus, to me, is like learning the poem by heart versus reading the lines in a book. Of course there is always room for improvement, but after dancing the stage routine, students, I have noticed, do hear, appreciate and dance out the uniqueness of each song in a much more expressive way. It makes them better dancers, which is exactly what we are after, isn't it?

Act III

Scene 2: *There's a Test!?!*

> *"Dance first. Think later.*
> *It's the natural order."*
> Samuel Beckett

Part 1. Check Out

Both Joan and I were surprised by what is involved in learning to dance. Of course our original impetus for taking dance lessons was dancing socially at the parties and functions we attended. I'd envisioned two or three months of lessons, learn the basic steps and then we could dance. Indeed, those basics steps came easily, providing a false sense of security of what was to follow.

Instead, we discovered a philosophy and methodology

of learning dance that we weren't ready for. Rather than simply clutching one another and moving our feet to the requisite points in time with the music, we were being taught to truly dance with style. What started out as a few lessons to learn some dance steps evolved into a dedicated study of the art form.

There is a methodical structure to teaching and learning dance. And there are recognized and accepted levels of demonstrated dance proficiency. As someone who has worked in management I wasn't surprised by this structure and methodology.

At the beginning of our dance studies Joan and I were entered into the Bronze I curriculum. There is an entire hierarchy of dance levels from Bronze to Gold with various levels in each category: Bronze I, Bronze II, Silver I, etc. Each level requires the mastery of specific dance moves. So, in addition to learning to simply perform the requisite steps in time to the music, we were being taught the style and techniques necessary to become Bronze Level I certified dancers.

There is a management axiom, "What gets measured, gets managed." Natasha and Lee manage our dance binder that records each lesson, what dance moves we've been taught, and our current proficiency with those moves. Woe to the student who tells Natasha, "I don't think we've done that," because out comes the annotated binder. More than once I've sheepishly recanted, "Oh, yea, you did show us that...could we go over it again?"

To insure the teaching and learning program is effective there is a two-part structured testing and certification process consisting of a 'check out' and a dancing exhibition before an Adjudicator.

In the 'check-out' Joan and I are required to demonstrate the specific moves associated with each of the dances we learned. And we have to do it without the comfort of each other's embrace. With Joan and I standing back-to-back, Natasha calls out the various steps, "basic Fox Trot," and execute the steps, in correct time, with the correct posture and frame. These moves are the 'school figures.' Consider it a hands-on proficiency exam such as anyone in a trade, craft or profession may have to perform to verify they have the requisite skill mastery. A Dance Master observes, grades the performance and provides feedback.

For those afflicted with any kind of performance anxiety, this process can be as harrowing as it sounds. Up until that time Joan and I always danced together, enjoying that "synergy of the whole is greater than the sum of the individual parts." I understand the necessity to demonstrate the individual competencies associated with each learned dance move, but that doesn't make it any less intimidating.

For two weeks prior to the check out, we devoted time during each lesson to learning to successfully perform these individual school figures. Finally Natasha decided we were ready to 'check out' and she scheduled the appointment.

Dancing With Natasha

Our check out was adjudicated by Radoslaw "Radek" Rogowski, a formidable dancer. As Joan and I performed our solo, silent, dance moves, Radek's practiced eye evaluated us. Sometimes we would be asked to repeat the moves, other times one demonstration was enough. Natasha called out the required moves, Joan and I nervously performed, and Radek observed, making notations on a long sheet of yellow paper.

Finally it was over; we'd passed our check out. Next was a short debriefing session, during which Radek addressed both our strengths and areas for improvement. His comments were quite on the mark, especially when he demonstrated the correct technique. The man can dance! Radek's notes were all in Polish, but based on how I felt about some of the moves in my check out, I wouldn't be surprised if they said something like, "Greg dances like he has a goat in his pants."

Part one of our Bronze I certification process was complete. The next step - the Dayton Dance Classic.

Part 2. Dance Wardrobe

Part two of our Bronze Level I certification took place at the Dayton Dance Classic, August 20, 2006. Joan and I would dance the: Cha-Cha, Fox Trot, Hustle, Mambo, Rumba, Swing, Tango and Waltz. Considering that we couldn't dance at all eight months earlier we felt that performing these eight dances in a ballroom, in front of other dancers, dance instructors, and an adjudicator who would critique our performance represented significant progress.

This event required two different dance costumes and formal wear for the dinner afterwards. The formal wear was no problem, I had a tuxedo and all the necessary accouterment, and Joan had the requisite gowns and accessories. But dance costumes? We'd need something semi-formal-glamorous for the smooth dances, the Waltz, Foxtrot and Tango, and we'd need something "showy" for the rhythm dances, the Rumba, Cha-Cha and Mambo.

Custom-made dance costumes are an expensive investment unless you are a competitive or professional dancer. Buying off-the-rack clothing suitable for dancing presents its own shopping dilemma. Women's gowns and cocktail dresses suitable for wear at a party may not be suitable for dancing. The fabric needs to drape providing room to flow. There must be unrestricted movement so the necessary under-arm turns and cross-over breaks can be executed.

Dance imposes some unique dynamics to the shopping process. We both have dance shoes; we bought those early into our lessons. But dance shoes are meant to be worn on the dance floor only; wearing them as street shoes will ruin them for dance. However, we quickly found that ordinary street shoes don't necessarily make for good dancing. This problem came to the fore when we started attending those very events that had prompted us to begin our dance lessons. We couldn't wear our dance shoes to a ball. One, it would ruin the shoes, and two, the dance shoes may not always be the most fashionable for the occasion. So the search was on for the compromise shoe: something that looks good with the outfit, has a smooth sole and provides the support required for dancing.

In a popular nation-wide store Joan and I searched for the right shoe to wear with the outfit to one of her events. As she tried on each shoe we would search for a space in the store and execute some dance moves: basic Rumba with an under-arm turn and a Swing with an American spin. This always brought smiles and bemused looks from the other customers and clerks. But it's the only way to know if the shoe will work. It's no longer enough to have a shoe that looks good and fits. Now we have to be able to dance in them as well.

And the same was true when Joan and I were shopping for her dresses in the mall. She would come out of the dressing room and we'd do a couple of dance moves. Could she turn in the dress, did her arms and legs have the necessary freedom of movement, did the fabric twirl and move in a pleasing way? These were critical considerations to be evaluated in any purchase.

Dance was changing our lives. It changed the way we listened to and heard the music around us; it changed how we used our leisure time; it was changing the way we shopped.

Joan had her performance wardrobe, but I was not so lucky. I had a white, formal shirt to wear with black pants for the smooth dances, but needed a matching vest and tie to complete the outfit. For the rhythm dances I wanted Latin flashy, something very Antonio Banderas or Ricky Ricardo.

I was still shopping for the right black slacks. For $29.95, the less than perfect pair, with belt loops, appeared. Joan performed a bit of belt-loop amputation to give them that Latin sexy line.

The local stores yielded nothing in the way of a vest and tie, but fate intervened. While doing a book signing in Cloumbus, Ohio, a trendy men's clothier was having a sale a few doors down. On the sidewalk was a rack of Hip-Hop / Gangsta styles. I was drawn like a fish to a lure toward a black shirt with silver glittery stripes. Yes, it was perfect for a Latin dance shirt, but it was too big.

"We have it in other sizes inside, at 40% off," said the clerk.

Inside I found said shirt in the perfect size, along with a shiny black shirt with embroidery on the front and cuffs. I also found two vests, with matching ties.

I got me a dance wardrobe! It's Showtime baby!

Dancing With Natasha

Part 3. Preparation

I have the most problem with dances that move around the floor in the line of dance, particularly the Foxtrot and Waltz. Corners are my downfall; managing the turns and working through the traffic, the other dancers on the floor, vexes me. I have more success with the dances that remain in one place: Swing, Cha-Cha, Rumba and Mambo. The Mambo, with its 'hold-on-the-one' syncopated rhythm also challenges me. Joan shakes her head in disbelief as I struggle with keeping the steps in time. "Take you out from behind the drum set and you have no rhythm," she exclaims. It's a true statement. Perhaps it's the old dance anxiety of being exposed and vulnerable on the floor.

The weeks leading up to the final part of our Bronze dance certification were a flurry of rehearsals, lessons and drills. We reviewed technique, stylistic moves, choreography, timekeeping, and what is called floorcraft, getting around the floor. Nearly every evening was spent at the studio for back-to-back lessons with Natasha or Lee: Tango, Hustle, Swing, Foxtrot, Waltz, Cha-Cha, Mambo and Rumba. Even Radek helped us polish up our Fox Trot grapevine and Tango moves.

The Tango flare promenade was a challenging move and poor Natasha *really* earned her dance instructor money working with me on the steps and timing on that one.

Gregory Causey

I was frustrated. The moves weren't coming naturally. I was still thinking about everything: remember the choreography, what move / step was coming next, how should we be positioned, what did I need to do to lead Joan, where was I on the floor, what did I have to do to transition from one spot to the next?

As a guitar player I don't think about how to play the chords in a song, where to put my fingers; I don't think about the timing, what to play, when. From experience it comes naturally. I'm still waiting for that to happen with dance, waiting for that automatic muscle memory, that instinct to kick in and take over. Until I get to that point I'm relying on memory, intellect and my abilities to plan and analyze. And as Natasha, Lee, Radek, Mario and the rest would tell you, that doesn't make for the most graceful and fluid of dance.

Natasha and Lee provided us with choreographed routines that incorporated all the moves necessary to complete our Bronze I certification. This relieved me of the need to think of 'what' to do, but we still had to execute it in a stylish manner. Lee worked with us on Hustle and Mambo. The Hustle is a fun dance, with an easy 4/4 beat. Lee's Mambo routine was more complex: basic step, arm check, back breaks, chase and spin, cross-body lead, cross-over break with a fifth position and a scallop, and back to the basic move. Whew!

Natasha's Tango wasn't any better: turning rocks

with corte', shadow rocks, basic with a promenade ending, triple fans, tango rocks and the dreaded flare promenade.

And so it went, with each dance we endeavored to have a plan to showcase our dancing skills to the event adjudicator.

Towards the end of the two-week marathon running up to the event Natasha could see the strain that Joan and I were under. She cut some of the lessons short. As a good instructor she wanted to get us to our peak (whatever that was) and keep us on that performing edge without over-training us. On the last Saturday morning before the event we went to the studio and ran through each dance under her watchful eye. She pronounced us ready to go and sent us on our way. Tomorrow would be the big day.

Part 4. "Is that my puddle?"

The big day, the Dayton Dance Classic, both Joan and I had a sense of...worry, foreboding, fear? All the above?

Joan was glamorous in her long burgundy gown, but then she started removing it, undressing. "What are you doing?" I asked.

"I'm not going."

We were both wary about dancing, performing in this structured and judged environment. Was she really

NOT going? What if...but...if she...

She smiled, "I'm just changing my girdle."

OK, we were still going. I got our bag o' dance shoes and our various costumes, and loaded everything in the car.

We'd attended the previous Dayton Dance Classic, but only as spectators...today would be different. The event was glamorous, a well appointed ballroom in Middletown, Ohio, beautiful ladies in gowns, hors' de oeuvres, and, most importantly for my mental well being and dance courage...the bar. We deposited our things at our table and adjourned to the changing rooms to don our dance shoes.

Our table was occupied by dance instructors Natasha and Svetlana, four other dance students, and Joan and I. Throughout the day we would all be getting up and down at different times to take the dance floor and display our skills.

There was still time before the festivities officially started and Natasha ushered us onto the floor to warm up. This dance floor was much larger than the studio, and it didn't have the same 'feel.' The floor at the studio was smooth and polished, our dance shoes moved easily across its surface. The floor of this ballroom was not as smooth, it felt slower and 'sticky,' it required more effort to execute our steps. Before, as a non-dancer, I never noticed such things. But now that I could dance, and I owned actual dance shoes, these things became apparent.

Dancing With Natasha

Joan and I danced through some of our routines. We tried to get a feel for where to start, how to approach the corners and relative distances, although I was pretty sure that such planning and dance reconnaissance would go out the window once we were on the floor being judged. Finally the music subsided, and everyone was invited to take their seats and get ready for the event to unfold before us.

As we sat at our table the sense of impending dance doom must have been apparent on my face. Natasha attempted to console me by saying that she would send Joan and I, "A beam of golden light." Obviously this was an instruction technique I was unaware of, perhaps taught to her by a mysterious Dance Guru in some late night ritual conducted in the dark recesses of the studio.

The overall structure of the event was confusing, at least to me. There were Heats of Closed and Open competitions. Natasha explained that we were competing against the dance standard and not the other dancers. The Closed competitions meant that dancers could only use those dance moves associated with their specific dance category (Bronze I, Bronze II, Silver I, etc.), whereas Open competition allowed dancers to use moves from any category. That didn't assuage my fears. Joan chimed in with the fact that she'd, "Been sick only once today."

Ever the optimistic revolutionary Natasha countered

my fears by saying, "We're like the proletariats, nothing to lose but our chains." My confidence suitably bolstered, I was ready to dance, or overthrow the capitalist bourgeoisie in Middletown, Ohio.

Joan looked at me at times asking me what was going on, as if I had any idea. "I don't know, we just wait and line up and dance what we're told." Sure enough, the time came and Natasha directed us to the end of the floor.

Joan and I stood there, watching the other dancers on the floor. We were next. If it was possible, the dance floor had grown. As we stood and watched I turned to Joan, and took her hand. Our eyes met. I looked at the floor and said, "Is that my puddle?" We cracked up; the tension subsided, if only for that brief moment.

The first dances were the smooth ones: Fox Trot, Waltz, and Tango. We didn't do as well as we would have wanted; we'd definitely danced better. But this part was over. We both breathed a sigh of relief and went for some refreshments.

Joan and I watched the other dancers take the floor, and wondered why we weren't dancing with the Novice groups. We were beginners, this was our first certification. We didn't know why we weren't dancing, we were merely reacting to the external stimuli around us: Natasha would say it was time to dance, send Joan and I out on the floor, and we'd dance the dance required.

Dancing With Natasha

On our second attempt at the Tango, Joan and I actually managed to get around the floor, sticking to our routine, even executing the dreaded Flare Promenade. This excited Natasha who screamed, clapped, and immediately startled us so that we lost our place in the routine. Ah…such are the trials of dance.

As the medals were handed out we were called up for Bronze I and Intermediate Bronze II. Bronze II? Weren't we competing as beginners, novices? Well, yes and no. It seems we were mistakenly entered into the higher level by mistake and it couldn't be changed. Natasha felt it better not to tell us, feeling the added pressure might freak us out. Well…YEAH!

Eventually the first phase was finished and we could change costumes, and prepare for those Rhythm dances I was looking forward to. Not that I'm great at those, but they don't move around the floor in the line of dance; I get to stay in one place.

Joan and I were more relaxed now, the original anxiety and nervousness fading as we grew more comfortable on the floor. We started enjoying ourselves. The Swing Heat seemed to go on forever; they re-started the music and told us to, "Keep dancing." Somehow we made it through the day, and Mario presented us with our Bronze I and Intermediate Bronze II certificates.

The entire event lasted several nine hours. It was a long and eventful day, full of fear, trepidation, joy and accomplishment. When it was over we were physically and mentally spent. It was the culmination of eight months and countless hours of work. There's no standard rate of progress in learning dance. People learn at their own pace according to their commitment and abilities. But Joan and I felt good. In eight months we had progressed from dance illiteracy to participation in the Dayton Dance Classic.

Yes, our Bronze dance certificates are proudly framed and displayed in our home.

18 February 2007

It's been six months since we participated in our first Dayton Dance Classic. This second one was much easier and more fun. We knew what to expect and we were more comfortable dancing with each other, and in front of others. We were among fellow dancers and friends.

We did seven dances this day, in both the Open and Closed categories, for a total of fourteen. For our efforts we received thirteen first place finishes and one second place, for our Closed Mambo, (Natasha said we had a problem with timing). Even our Waltz, which had given me the most trouble, garnered a "With Honors" placing. Mid-way through the program we took the floor and danced the required dances (Cha-Cha, Swing, Foxtrot and Waltz) for our full medal checkout from the Bronze II certification program.

The Adjudicator, Terry Irwin, stopped by our table to congratulate us. He'd seen us dance when we attended our first Dayton Dance Classic as spectators only, a year ago. He told us that we'd done well and were the most improved dancers on the floor.

Considering that a scant fourteen months ago we couldn't dance at all, I had to agree. During a break for open dancing, as Joan and I were on the floor, she looked at me and said, "Can you believe we're dancing?"

Yes, as a matter of fact, I can.

Gregory Causey

$\mathcal{N}atasha...$

On Dance Certification

The very first graduation ball I attended was held in the studio, where half of the floor was occupied with chairs, the other half was left for dancing – and it still seemed huge to me. I had single student graduating from Bronze I. So little did I know about what was my role, that when the student started Cha-Cha on beat three instead of one, I let him...after all it's his skills that were graded, right? That was the last in-studio graduation ball ever, because the very next one we were dancing on the spacious floor of Manchester Inn, historical hotel in Middletown, Ohio, whose ballrooms are known for hosting big bands in the season. And yes, the floor at Manchester is slower than the one we have in the studio, but to me it's better than the faster one – which Greg would probably call slippery.

When the students begin working on the medal program, all they know about their goals is what we say would match their dreams and desires. They can't possibly have enough information to make elaborate choices about their dancing. Reminds me of professor's question, "Do you have any questions?" to the student who just spent hour and a half madly scribbling the lecture down, trying not to miss one word. What questions? Let me decipher what I scribbled first!

Actually, keeping the analogy, since we are the teachers and they are the students, their only natural question should be not if there's a test, but WHEN is the test.

As it is done throughout all Arthur Murray studios we have two graduations a year. It seems perfectly logical, considering that we have two festivals a year, at which time we revise the individual programs and set the new goals for the students. And just like in any other school, before we set new goals we need some proof that the previous ones were successfully met. I can make a callus on my tongue praising some of the students for great progress, and they will still think they…ummm…are not good enough, unless someone of higher authority, someone who doesn't work with them every week, someone whose digestion is not going to be affected by whether they are happy or not is going to tell them that they indeed are good enough to meet the standards.

I do take pride in the high standards of dancing that Arthur Murray International, Inc. is so adamant about. Quality is expected – and regularly checked on. As the teachers get certified for each level, so do students – fair is fair, hence Dayton Dance Classic (DDC). At least the students have to know only their own parts in the pattern, whereas the teachers must learn both man's and lady's parts. Both parts, with all details, in roughly 300 patterns in Full Bronze, the test will be in 6 months – how would you like that for a little dance pressure?

If it were just a little get-together in the studio, perhaps they wouldn't get so nervous for the first time, but we are talking big gala, the whole day event, with the adjudicator perched above the crowd seeing everything. It's glamorous, it's unnerving, it's motivating – I swear I didn't book all the lessons Greg and Joan put in one month before DDC – they did it of their own free will. What such a dance marathon before the event is good for – besides propelling the anxiety – it makes clear for the students as well as the teacher where they have good solid base and what is fluff, something not yet fully absorbed. After so many DDC's since that first graduation ball I mentioned, I still believe that students should be prepared to dance what they really know and not what they could grasp in a hurry at the last moment – then the whole event is much more enjoyable for them and gives much more satisfaction to the teacher.

Great! Now how do you explain that to newcomers? Nobody had confirmed to them yet what it is they really know. They don't know the drill. The structure of event is unfamiliar to them. Their eyes helplessly wander not knowing where to focus, and they ask the same question over and over just because they can't concentrate enough to hear the answer. I know that once they hit the floor they will have hot and cold spells, they will feel naked and exposed, they will sweat and shiver, they will forget every single word of advice and encouragement I gave them – and only good solid base, the muscle memory, is going to save them from getting helplessly tangled in their own feet. I also know at this moment they would much rather run away, and perhaps the only thing that keeps them from doing so is the prospect of facing me.

How do I know all this? Well, I did have my first graduation ball, didn't I? Which leads me to believe that by the next time around my precious-in-their-nervousness 'babies' will answer more questions than they will be asking, will know what exactly the difference is between Open and Closed categories, and will be able to smile as they dance because they already know what they are doing.

Act III

Scene 3: The Big Show

*"To watch us dance is
to hear our hearts speak."*
Hopi Indian Saying

The studio puts on a show every year, a dance extravaganza replete with stage, props, lighting, music, choreography and wonderful dancing. It gives all those wanna-be performers a chance to live out their dance dreams.

The show is a tradition started by Barbara and Tim Haller. It gives the students and professionals a chance to stretch out and challenge themselves and their dance skills. There are solo, ensemble and couple's performances. The students have the opportunity to develop a dance routine with a professional choreographer and perform it with another student or a professional. It goes without saying that a lot of time is devoted to such a project. The planning for each year's show begins shortly after the current one.

Natasha attempted to talk me into performing in the 2006 production, as a member of the 'men's number.' However, my dance fears and anxieties were not yet fully assuaged for me to 'show off' in such a manner. The show went on without me, and unfortunately Joan and I were out of town when it was performed. But I did see a DVD of the performance and was very impressed.

During the first six months of 2006, as Joan and I began our dance journey, we'd see pieces of rehearsals in the studio. Saturdays were always a good time for people to get together to practice the larger ensemble numbers. In the evenings as Joan and I took lessons, we'd see couples working on their routines. Often they'd stop and review a video tape of the moves. Throughout the year the choreographer, Terry Irwin, would visit the studio to help the dancers hone their numbers.

The show was performed in July 2006, at a college auditorium, providing the perfect setting, allowing the performers to work on a real stage. Called *Curtain's Up*, it replicated the feel of a stage show in production.

While the Friday night practice parties at the studio give everyone a chance to put all those lessons to use, the annual show takes it an order of magnitude beyond. Choreographed, costumed and bathed in the floodlights, the dancers literally take center stage. For the duration of the song, they create the energy that flows to the audience, is amplified and is given back to them. There is immediacy, a "you-had-to-be-there" quality to that energy, that you don't get from watching a video.

But viewing the video gave me an appreciation for the work that went into the production, and the technique and styling evidenced in the performances. I witnessed levels of dance and moves from my fellow students that I'd not seen in the studio.

Natasha performed a passionate and sultry Rumba with her student Pete. Lee and his student Linda danced an exquisite and beautiful Bolero. Natasha and Joe staged a touching Tango from *Scent of a Woman*. Lee and his professional partner Melissa Neeley took *Pink Floyd's "Hey You"* to a new artistic level with their evocative dance interpretation. Svetlana and Mario entertained everyone with a fun and energetic Polka. Mario and Joann had the house rocking with their jump and jive swing number, *Big Fun*. Paula performed a solo number, her smooth and supple lines in her flowing white dress holding the audience captive in rapt attention.

The show was well paced, with light-hearted numbers effectively interspersed by dramatic and evocative pieces. The closing number was performed by the studio professional staff. It was a high-energy affair that let the pros show off their dance skills and it brought the evening to a fitting close.

A curtain call brought each performer out for a final bow, one last accolade from an appreciative and enthusiastic audience. I couldn't help but reflect for a moment that many of the great routines I'd just witnessed on the video had been performed by students, people like myself, who months, or years earlier had walked through those same studio doors with nothing but the desire to learn to dance. Some may have been searching for that outlet, had the desire to be on the stage, to be in a show. Perhaps others, once infused with the beauty, power and elegance of dance, felt that fire kindled within them. Whatever the motive, dance opened up that performance avenue to these people, allowing them a forum for their creative expression.

I was curious now about the show, and when the studio began putting together the next event I wanted to see how it all begins. I attended a Saturday morning rehearsal as they started to walk through and choreograph the opening number.

I settled in with my notebook, digital camera and

bottle of water and watched as the participants milled around on the dance floor. There were people in slacks and shirts, jeans, sweat suits, all wearing dance shoes, some stretching and loosening up. It looked very "chorus line, dance gypsy" and I'm sure that many felt some tingling of excitement about the many weeks and months ahead leading to the final performance.

The choreographer, Terry Irwin, placed people in their positions on the dance floor. There was a feeling of excitement...until the music started. The music for the opening number was *It's a Small World*. The horror, the horror! I can't imagine weeks and months of rehearsing to THAT song. It's one of those tunes that gets in your head and repeats itself, all day, endlessly, until... Some songs are like that, annoying, through no fault of their own. Even a Reggae / Calypso version of *It's a Small World*, as this one was, can't save one from the spell it casts. Wishing my water bottle held something infinitely stronger I girded my authorial loins and settled in to capture the events to unfold before me.

It's a small world after all.

With the people in place, some holding flags, Terry began guiding them through their movements. He told them to march like ducks, designating some of them as, "Mama ducks," and, "Head ducklings." With a shortage of people on this particular number he motioned for the, "Flag girls, come in and be a duck for a minute."

Dancing With Natasha

It's a small world after all.

There followed much walking through of the parts and steps, starts and stops, and counting beats and measures to ensure the choreography matched the appropriate places in the music. Clearly, great dance performances don't just happen, but are planned, developed and honed, although one must never discount luck. At one point Terry said, "I didn't plan on that, but sometimes the dance Gods smile on me."

It's a small world after all.

Terry worked the group on positioning, speed and step length, marking spots, "When I come on...when I come toward." The music was repeated so the proper lyric cues could be sequenced with the steps. Terry observed and identified problems, working out ways to get people to the right locations at the right times. He was working it out in real time, where and when to put the people. Before long the group was moving, making circles, intertwining, turning and intersecting; with the flags it all had a marching band feel. Terry kept working to make it, "Visually more active...one-two-three-Hit!, one-two-three-Hit!" Sometimes the directions were a bit vague, as when he said, "The outside line will do 'something' with their flags for eight counts."

It's a small, small world

Through it all, Terry kept it light, using humor to take the edge off any rehearsal stress. He noted that,

"Lee's not here to bug me today," which got a laugh from the crowd. And when he asked, "Joseph, how's your break dancing?" everyone, including Joseph, cracked up.

It's a small world after all.

As all of this was happening there was a new couple in the small ballroom having their beginning dance lesson. An entire cycle of dance was unfolding before my eyes, beginners, pros, and people working to pursue their dance dreams.

I watched as Svetlana ended her private lesson and walked to the front of the studio. As she walked down the dance floor her body moved to the music of the show rehearsal. I don't know if she was consciously doing this or it was simply a matter of her dancer's natural instinct reacting to the external aural and rhythmic stimuli. Regardless of the reason, I was fascinated at how easily she fell into moving with the music. Was this our dancer's goal, our Holy Grail, to become one with the music, to feel it everywhere and react to it naturally?

Terry wrapped up the rehearsal session telling everyone, "I think that's enough to confuse us for awhile." It was over, but it was a beginning. Walking to my car I felt sure that with expert coaching and hard work it would be a smashing number.

It's a small world after all.
It's a small world after all.

As this book is going to press I finally succumbed to Natasha's entreaties and allowed myself to be signed up for the "men's number" in the 2007 show. Famed choreographer Terry Irwin will direct the number, *Beautiful Girls*. Joan doesn't plan to be in the show, but she tells me she will be part of the enthusiastic audience.

Gregory Causey

ℕatasha...

On The Big Show

The show! If you have ever played the theater you will understand the excitement even the word brings. It's all behind – the technical rehearsal, the dress rehearsal, endless repetitions, searching for costumes, searching for the image, polishing it off, refining, refining again... It's all behind, it's seven o'clock on Saturday night and from the stage you can hear, softened by the heavy curtains, voices of the audience...before you dance the only thought is, *Why do I do this to myself?*, and after it's over you know why. Because it's beautiful, because it's elating, because it takes everything you know and makes you into the star – because it's theater.

Sometimes we get to dance the show routines more than once – take them to competition, present them at the graduation ball, or re-visit it once more on the stage – but for most it's this one starry night, one of a kind performance, never to be seen again. It's a wonderful opportunity for those who like this kind of game – I mean besides the benefits of becoming better dancers.

I was just a beginner teacher when the idea of replacing the traditional show-case with the staged show came about, but I remember everyone felt very enthusiastic about it. We started in the old theater, Sorg Opera House in Middletown, Ohio, and stayed there for several years until the opportunity presented itself to try the stage of the Memorial Hall in Dayton. When the Memorial Hall was closed Tim and Barbara Haller took us to the Finkleman Auditorium at Miami University, Middletown – and the friendship with this theater has been very fruitful ever since.

Usually the next show marathon starts on the wave of excitement of the previous one. We have the permanent cast, so to speak – students who danced in almost all of the shows, and these would be the ones to sign up for the next show routine almost immediately. They usually know already what they are after – the certain music, certain dance, certain theatrical elements – it's all piled up and presented to choreographer Terry Irwin, who knows them well – how they learn, how they perform, how they feel – and, more important, how they want to feel and look on the stage.

Next ones to sign in are students who actually have watched the previous show and were inspired by it. There's something to be said about the privilege of being personally acquainted with the performers – when they see the fellow students looking great on the stage, the desire to try it too comes naturally, I guess. These people usually have their cherished favorite song they would like to dance to – and it's our job to fit it smoothly into the theme of the next show.

There are traditional ladies and men's numbers – those would be picked to suit the overall theme of the show, but typically the ladies number would be some very feministic variety type, and men's number traditionally is thought as the comedy where our gentlemen, whether single or married, bond through masculine humor. Couple's number sometimes pair people who don't dance together other than occasionally at the parties – and that is great training in leading and following. Opening number is open to everyone who works on the medal program, no matter how experienced – and it is very closely tied to the theme of the show, so we can come up with music for it as soon as the theme of the next show is decided on.

Between all of the above, plus a couple of professional numbers, plus visiting performers, two thirds of the show are in the works – and that is when the newbies are getting recruited. What does it take to talk the newbies into dancing on the stage? Hmmm...lots of talking – yet it's hard to talk someone into feeling confident that it's going to be all right if they have never been on stage before. Demonstration of the video of one of the previous shows might work – but the video is usually lacking the charm of the live performance, and may not be as convincing. As a matter of fact I know many dancers, students and professionals alike, who were very critical of their performance after watching the tape. To this, by the way, there is a prescription by Terry Irwin, "Let it sit there for couple of months, then watch it again." The logic of this advice is simple – time helps to detach us from all the expectations we were putting on our performance, and allows us to see ourselves with the eyes of the spectator, to enjoy the story being unfolded.

So here we are back to telling the story – and that is the winning argument in talking to the newbies. Everyone has a story to tell, and if we invite people to tell their story and show how it can be done – they will take the risk. I used to work with a couple who first came into the studio soon after their tenth wedding anniversary – and I remember just to watch them being in love like newlyweds was making my day. So when talking about the show I knew exactly the music – the Habanera from all-about-worshipping-the-woman movie "Don Juan de Marco." I don't think our discussion whether to do it or not took longer than five minutes – I played the music and it was decided. By the way, they celebrated their eleventh anniversary and twelfth too, right on the stage of Sorg Opera House, dancing in the show.

To the very artistic young man who came into the

studio, as he told us, to "Meet higher quality women," we offered to dance "Mona" – a little Rumba from "Class Act" that starts with the blunt announcement, "Talent always turns me on." Well, for our routine we had to turn the original, "young talented writer," into a "young talented artist," just because the student who was dancing is a draftsman, and besides it was telling the story better, but it paid off – young man felt much more in his element, and even came up with the portrait of Mona, which is still adorning the wall in my living room.

"You've got to change your evil ways, baby," turned into entertaining Cha-Cha for the lady who's cool sharp wit was admired by everyone.

The man who came on his first lesson in cowboy boots and loved to spend time with the numerous friends in the numerous bars danced "Trashy Woman" with yours truly. It was the last show where Tim and Barbara Haller danced with us and for us, and so the cast included some friends of theirs who came to pay tribute to the great dancers. One of them was Roy Stone, the coach and choreographer from Florida. At the cast party after the show Roy came to me with one of the biggest compliments I have ever received about my performance. See, the trashy woman ain't pretty, her clothes are disarrayed, she is tipsy to say the least, and besides she had to periodically relieve her nose into the huge white handkerchief that was casually stuffed into her bosom. Besides very heavy makeup that was needed for the character there was no disguise on me – it was still me blowing nose, smiling drunken smile, stumbling, falling – to the greatest delight of the audience. So when Roy came to express his respect for courage to put myself out in such light I felt flattered, perhaps because Roy knew where I started. He was the one who once spent forty-five minutes making me repeat one and same gesture – over the head, down the neck, through the cleavage out to the side. He was trying so hard to help me to get out of my shell – only to see me stiffening and blushing miserably over and over on the cleavage part.

Of course the ability to express the emotions, to sell the story, is the most important for the stage. As we say to our students, the audience doesn't know what the choreography is, so even if you make a mistake – make it part of the dance and move on. (Easier said than done – takes couple mistakes to live through). Next thing is projecting. We rehearse our routines in the studio, surrounded by mirrors that are faithfully reflecting the subtle motions, half smiles and small gestures, making us believe it looks good. It's hard to imagine that stage would require five times that much, it's also hard to force ourselves so far out of our habitual personal space – the space we're accustomed to in everyday life. Especially if we don't have a frame of reference. What does it mean when the teacher and the coach keep saying, "Make it bigger." Bigger? How exactly big should be bigger if what

I do now already feels huge and obnoxious? As a result people sometimes get disappointed when watching their first performance on video. I was too at first – but being a teacher gives me luxury of a new chance at least once a year. Gradually moving from always feeling like catching the falling plates to being confident that it is going to look pretty darn close to what choreographer had in mind, to actually enjoying the dance, to living the story here and now – it was quite a quest. I think there are some of our students from show veterans who can say the same thing about themselves. What I personally have learned for sure in the process is to always teach my student partner how to lead – because, even though I have been on the stage on and off all my life, I have severe case of stage fright, and tend to space out every now and then right in the middle of the dance. I do warn about this up-front though – makes a great motivation.

One of the most beautiful things about the show is the camaraderie that is reigning in the wings. At first everyone works on their routine privately, scheduling lessons when the studio is not too crowded, when the time allows breaks and contemplations on the character. Closer to the show there may be two-three routines at once sharing the floor and the music time. Then Thursday comes, the day when we mark the stage and do first technical rehearsal – and from then on, until the last guest leaves the traditional cast party late Saturday night, all participants are going to be like one family. They will carry the props in and out of the theater. They will willingly step in as the stage hands for one another. They will make the dressing assembly line if someone needs quick change between the numbers. They will help each other with the makeup, hair styling, cold drinks, pins, ties, snacks, hair blowers, shoe laces and whatever else might be needed at the last moment, including looking for lost-on-the-premises partner, warm hugs and the words of encouragement. If you are going on the stage, you can be sure there will be someone who'll wish you to break the leg – and someone who'd meet you with the, "Great job!" and high-five once you got back in the wings. Most of the time they won't talk about their emotions before dancing – only endless pacing, rubbing hands, fidgeting with the costumes will show how nervous they are – but once the curtain is finally down there's usually a great victorious scream of relief and happiness that this is over – no one cares that the people in the audience can still hear us – hallelujah, it's done!!

Next week we'll start all over again. But it's going to be next week.

Act III

Scene 4: Denouement

*"Dancing is the loftiest, the most moving,
the most beautiful of the arts, because it is not mere
translation or abstraction from life;
it is life itself."*
Havelock Ellis

After months of lessons I found myself alone one weekend while Joan was on a business trip. Joan and I are very much in the habit of going to the studio on Friday and dancing. The idea of an evening home alone, when I could be out dancing was not appealing, but to go alone? I called Joan and told her that I was thinking about it. "Go dance," she said. So I did.

In the months before I started lessons I would have never had the confidence to ask a woman to dance, especially one who was not my wife. But that night I approached each woman and politely asked, "Would you like to dance?" and they graciously accepted. Throughout the evening I danced with most of the women in attendance, doing a mix of Rumba, Cha-Cha, Foxtrot, Swing and Hustle. There were instances when the pros, Svetlana, Natasha or Justyna found me and brought me on the floor. I stayed until the end, the final dance, when Mario put on a Polka. I turned to leave the floor, but was stopped by Natasha.

She grabbed my hand. "Come on, we'll Polka."

"I...uh...I don't know how..." It was another case of total dance immersion. Natasha grabbed me and we literally flew around the floor. While I attempted to execute the basic footwork she turned and whirled as we kept our frantic circular pace. Finally the song ended, the evening was over.

When I look back on that night I can see many of the themes of this book echoed in that brief evening encounter. I had the confidence to go into a social situation and perform in front of others. Oh, and I had fun.

So what does it all mean? What can we surmise from the preceding pages? While writing this book, I discovered several common themes. Regardless of whether the person is a beginner, a more advanced student, or a seasoned dance professional many find that dance gives them the same things. Dance isn't simply something that we do; it has the power to be something that becomes us. Dance can literally change our lives.

Gregory Causey

Fun is the descriptor I heard often when talking to people about dance. Whether it's the joy of accomplishment, the endorphin rush from the sheer physicality, the way they surrender to the music, or the performance itself, people who dance, enjoy it. Joan's face lights up when we dance; she laughs, she smiles.

Dance can be the pathway to build the confidence to develop a skill and display it before others. I've witnessed men and women walk in the studio, dressed in their work clothes. With a change of shoes and a step onto the dance floor they are transformed. In dance we have permission to express ourselves. The plumber becomes a 40's Jitterbug Hep Cat. The accountant becomes a sensual seductress.

Ballroom dance is a social medium, a community. At the dance studio one is taken into that community, made a part of that social network. Whatever their other interests or socio-economic backgrounds everyone shares a love of dance. This common ground provides a basis for cultivating new acquaintances and friendships. Removed from the confines of the studio ballroom dance continues its social impact. At weddings and parties the opportunity to dance can be an ice breaker, a way to meet others and engage in a socially acceptable practice...dancing.

Dances such as the Quick Step, Mambo, Samba, Viennese Waltz and Swing are physically demanding. Dancing can help people get in shape and stay that way.

And this doesn't apply to only the body. Learning new steps and memorizing new routines provides mental stimulation that continually hones our cognitive skills.

Psychologist Abraham Maslow postulates that the human experience is a pyramid of successive needs that must be met. These begin with the most basic, survival, and proceed to self-actualization, wherein the individual realizes life's full potential. In between these two extremes are other human needs such as security, safety, socialization and self-esteem. Dance has the ability to fill many of these requirements. The exercise and physical benefits can certainly go a long way to insuring health and survival imperatives. The group interaction with other dance partners can fill social desires, and the dance performance aspect fills the quest for self-esteem. There are even those people who find their life's calling and self-actualize through the medium of dance.

Dance has the power to change lives. I've watched people of all sorts meet at the dance studio to dance, enjoy each other's company, have fun, show off, and burn calories. A year ago I couldn't have imagined dancing, or writing this book, but dancing has changed my life.

Gregory Causey

$\mathcal{N}$atasha...

On The Power of Dance

Once upon a time, way before I had enough teaching experience to see long term changes that can be achieved through dancing, a young man walked in the door. "I always wanted to learn how to dance," he announced, "and after the accident I figured – now is the time." He was quite noticeably limping, his arms and head in scars, wrists damaged, so naturally I asked him – what accident? "Well," he said, "I used to work in construction and took a free fall thirty-three feet to the ground. The flight was OK, but the landing could have been better."

So here he was – after months and months of being stitched back together and all kinds of therapies – to learn how to dance. It was…a struggle, because he had suffered so many injuries, he was afraid to move. We were working on social dancing for a couple of months, when the idea of doing a stage show came along. I knew that being on the stage requires one to pull together everything they have for the performance. So I decided to work around the young man's fears. I tricked him. He liked Swing and Jitterbug very much, but had a hard time dancing them. I suggested we do Jitterbug on the stage. His eyes lit up.

"It's going to be hard," I warned him.

"Fine," he said, "Let's do it."

The choreographer came to the studio, looked at us moving, and without saying much put together a short beginning for the routine. After the show was danced he confessed to me that he didn't think we would pull it off, and he thought I was, "Out of my mind to make the boy dance the Jitterbug on stage."

We did dance it just fine. It was admittedly one of the cutest numbers in the show. I had to push my future celebrity, sometimes hard too, but as a result his limp went almost unnoticeable, he got rid of the fear of using his body, and there was no woman in the studio who didn't love to dance with him for he did learn to lead. The routine was more of a comedy, and it gave him the opportunity to play again – after all he was still very young.

Ever since I have been big believer in great therapeutic effects of dance, and I dare to say that physical part of the healing is the least significant. I have learned that universal prescription from just about any wrongs that may happen to me is to get some dancing done. The beauty of this remedy is that it's always available – all you need is a dime of space and a good beat. You don't have to be good at it to enjoy moving with the beat, even though I have to say it again – being at least comfortable helps.

Another example of when dancing helped people to cope with their pain and confusion was the Friday night practice session that was held after September 11th. We debated for a long time if we should even open the doors, and finally decided to do it because we felt there could be some, our students, out there who wouldn't know where else to go. The crowd wasn't overly large that evening, but still the number of people who came was surprising, and everyone was very grateful for the opportunity to be with friends. The feeling of being united, of being one big family was overwhelming and very comforting in that time of grief. So when talking about the power dance lends to us, healing power would be the word.

There was a book by Lynn Grabhorn called *Excuse Me, Your Life is Waiting*, where to identify the core reason for our wishes and desires, the author was offering very simple method – she was asking one question – "Why?" She'd ask this question until layer after layer all the conventional reasoning is peeled off and the shiny "because it feels good" appears at the very bottom. So the bottom line is – ultimately, given the chance, dancing makes people feel good, whatever the official reason.

When people start learning to dance the results are always open-ended. Dancing strips people. By bringing them to an emotional zenith – whether it's state of elation or frustration, does not matter – it makes people feel open and vulnerable. I heard a comment once – "She dances with her soul stripped naked for everyone to see." Scary? Yes! However, come to think of it, as dancing makes us open and vulnerable in the same instance it gives us a permission to be such.

There are many beautiful, intriguing, unique sides of our multi-dimensional personalities that may never see the light otherwise, where dancing in time will inevitably bring them to this light. When we teach our students the character of the dance we are trying to show them how to let out these different sides of their personalities without feeling insecure. I think it's wonderful when in Rumba, for instance, you can be as sultry as you can muster – and get away with it, because it's a character of the dance. And when your partner in Swing lets out this spontaneous giggle just because it feels good – wasn't it worth the effort? Just imagine, all in one evening of dancing you are allowed to be anything you ever wanted to – and not only remain socially acceptable, but be in demand – just for being yourself. Where else is it possible?

It's not easy to get out of your shell. But the ease comes with the skill. Once you know you look cool enough even when playing silly, you can afford to play silly – and that is the freedom dance gives us.

Now, because dancing strips people to their naked soul, there may be some surprises, and they may be anywhere between pleasant to shocking, depending how aware you are of yourself and how much you are ready to discover about yourself. It is indeed life altering experience, and as such it doesn't always go the direction we, in our conditioned minds, would want it to go. But I choose to believe that it always takes us in the right direction, for dancing in its essence is the expression of joy of life, and what can possibly be wrong about joy?

Finale

We Can Dance!

*"There are short-cuts to happiness,
and dancing is one of them."*
Vicki Baum

December 8, 2006: The Headquarters Christmas Party; it's been nearly a year since we started taking dance lessons. Tonight Joan and I would attend her annual headquarters Christmas party.

At last year's party, we'd stepped nervously onto the floor, groped each other and shuffled our feet. When the obligatory dance was over, we quietly exited the floor and went home.

This year's party was a wonderful event, a cheerfully decorated ballroom, tasty buffet dinner and good camaraderie. There were funny moments, cute presentations and even an appearance by Santa. When the formal festivities finished, the DJ began. The music was a modern derivative hip-hop, but my now-trained dancing ear detected a Cha-Cha groove underlying the rhythm. Joan and I rose, taking the dance floor and employing as many moves as our memories and courage would allow. I couldn't help but notice people watching.

We claimed part of the dance floor and danced a lively Swing. At one point, one of Joan's colleagues who was dancing the usual non-couples party dancing, asked Joan, "What are you doing?" I guess they were intrigued by our spins, turns, cross-over breaks and walks and points. Joan simply replied that we were, "Ballroom dancing."

I wanted to dance a Rumba so I asked the DJ to play *Sway* by the *Pussycat Dolls*. Two songs later my request hit the rotation and Joan and I took the dance floor. No one else was dancing so we used the entire floor, slinking across in our Cuban walks, cross-over breaks, open-breaks with under-arm turns, swivels, everything we could do.

We danced away the evening, and as we began to leave, a woman rose from a nearby table and approached us. "Oh, you're not leaving are you? I've so enjoyed watching you dance."

On the way home from last year's party Joan and I discussed taking lessons so we could dance at these functions. We'd gone from standing and groping each other a year ago to: "I've so enjoyed watching you dance."

Gregory Causey

WE CAN DANCE.
WE LOVE TO DANCE!

Natasha, you've done well.
I want to thank you very much
for giving Joan and me the
Power of the Dance.

Encore

Curtain Call

A Menu of Words of Wisdom on Dance and Life by Natasha

Starters

Rotate.
Breathe.
Look at her.
Smaller steps.
Don't look at her.
Stay on your toes.

Favorites

OK, now make it sexy.
All men are Hedgehogs.
Be my girl, be good girl.
Now let's try it with a real woman.
That was beautiful...but dangerous.

Specialties

Finish the box.
Move your center.
Lead with your heels.
Where is line of dance?
Bring the feet together.
Drop the hand, just drop it.
Don't rotate, go straight back.

Classics

Grow to God.
Two…it comes after one.
Make it easy on yourself.
Look to infinity and beyond.
Love the floor, love the woman, love yourself.
You don't have to love me; you just have to learn to dance.

Principle Cast Photographs

Natasha Yushanov

*Dayton Arthur Murray Dance Studio Manager,
Dance Professional and Author*

Photo by Bob Baemel

Lee Burchett

Dance Professional

Photo by Bob Baemel

Mario Kraszewski

Owner Dayton Ohio
Arthur Murray Dance Studio

Photo by Bob Baemel

Svetlana Hollenbaugh

Dance Professional

Photo Courtesy of Svetlana Hollenbaugh

Justyna Masajlo
And
Radoslaw "Radek" Rogowski

Dance Professionals

Photo by Judy Grigsby

Paula Kirkland

Dance Professional

Photo by Judy Grigsby

Principle Cast

Listed Alphabetically

These are the professionals, teachers and performers, who share their talents and love of the art so that all may experience the power and freedom of dance.

Lee Burchett

Smooth, that's the word that comes to mind when I think of Lee, or watch him dance. Tall, good looking, with dark hair: in white tie and tails he would be the perfect addition for a Cary Grant movie from the 40's. And that's such an incredible juxtaposition to the same Lee that roars up to the dance studio in a leather jacket on his motorcycle. Truly, dance people come in all varieties. But on the dance floor he moves effortlessly; women float in his arms. He exudes power and control with grace and style.

Surprisingly, Lee has only been dancing since

1997. Watching him move on the floor it's hard to imagine him not having a background of decades of dance, other than two semesters in college. Self-described, Lee was a, "Long-haired, artistic, intellectual type."

A college dance classmate told him the local Arthur Murray studio had lost one of their teachers and were in the market for a male dance instructor. Finding only two shirts with buttons in his closet, he settled on one and went for the interview. After a conversation with Barbara Haller, they danced. Though she entered him into the four month training program, he was teaching only two months later.

This illustrates the extreme diversity and the ways that people come to teach. Lee literally walked in off the street with nothing but the desire to learn and a shirt with buttons.

Lee explained that most of his development stemmed from the literally thousands of hours he and his dance partner, Melissa Neeley, practiced for dance competitions. They competed in Chicago, Cleveland, Nashville, Lexington, and Los Angeles. Working with professional trainers and coaches they eventually became successful enough to support their 'dance habit' with their very expressive style.

Lee credits two professional dance coaches, Terry Irwin and Ed Simon, with much of his development as a dancer and teacher. Terry Irwin helped Lee refine his own technical skills, teaching him how to explain dance concepts and techniques in ways that students could easily understand them.

Ed Simon was the primary coach for Lee and his partner Melissa Neeley when they were competing. Ed helped Lee make the jump from watching someone and being able to tell if they were 'good or bad' dancers, to being able to analyze 'why' a person was the kind of dancer they were.

As a benefit of dance Lee cites, "Happiness, people are happy when they dance." He echoed other pros who mentioned confidence, which Lee says, "Comes by forcing yourself into uncomfortable situations and succeeding."

Another benefit, according to Lee, is the personal contact that comes from dancing. Lee explains that one of the most important needs of small children is the need to be touched, and that we all retain that need for human contact.

Lee said he likes teaching and working with couples, watching as those walls that society and the pressures of work and life build start to fall away on the dance floor. He likes to, "Watch couples start to enjoy each other." When he's having a bad day he, "puts those negative thoughts and feelings aside and concentrate on my students...helping people always makes me feel better."

On a more personal, self-fulfillment level, Lee confessed that what he likes about dancing is, "Showing off, being good at something and being acknowledged for it." His favorite style is, "Whatever I'm dancing at the moment. It's best when you're in a dance and you get your muse; it feeds on itself."

He was once in a show with a relatively new dancer, a woman who had experienced some personal hardships and had recently found the joys of dancing. During their performance she became nervous, but Lee remained in control, and fed by his strength and confidence she finished the program. Afterwards she hugged him, confessing that it had been one of the best times of her life, something she'd done just for herself.

Barbara Haller

Had I known of Barbara's impressive dance pedigree I would have excused myself from her invitation to Waltz at the first Dayton Dance Classic Joan and I attended. At that early point in my dance education I'd have been too scared to dance with such a renowned artist. But Barbara was gracious and sympathetic to a dancing 'newbie.'

At the age of five, Barbara began ballet lessons, and realized over time, "I had been given a gift from God, the talent to dance."

Immersing herself in dance she continued to hone her craft until she was thirteen. At that time she was one of a handful of New York/New England area students selected for an intensive dance training educational program. This program found her attending conventional academic classes in the morning and an arts and dance curriculum in the afternoon and evenings. She studied dance, choreography, makeup and any number of theatrical subjects.

At the conclusion of these studies she joined the dance company of dance icon Rudolph Nuereyev and toured Europe, remaining there for the next five years. Returning to the United States to help promote ballet dancewear a friend offered, "If you ever get tired of dancing on your toes, call me." At that point Barbara was ready to try something else.

Her ballroom inspiration came when she saw the world-class theatrical dance performance of Pierre Dulaine. The years spent as a classically-trained ballet dancer were about to lead Barbara into a new realm of success and personal achievement. The next few years saw Barbara become a successful dance studio owner and achieve national acclaim as a four-time National Theatrical Arts Dance champion.

As with other people interviewed for this book, Barbara has strong feelings about the benefits of dance. She said she has witnessed countless couples, whose relationships have been strengthened and enhanced by dance, couples who now, "Focus on each other." One long-time couple still dance at the studio founded by Barbara; they perform in every show and their children dance as well. They told Barbara, "Thank you so much, it's the best thing we've ever done for each other."

What does Barbara like best about dance? To her, it's the ability to, "Make people 'feel' and see their reactions to the joy it brings them." A quote from Helen Keller keeps Barbara motivated every day: "The best and most beautiful things in life can not be seen or ever touched, they must be felt with the heart."

Her favorite style of dance, among all those that she has mastered, is the theatrical, ballroom style, although for social dancing she does favor the Cha-Cha.

It's her love of people and her belief that we are, "social animals," that led her to teaching dance. She loves getting to know people and freely admits to, "Learning more from students than they've learned from me." As an acclaimed performer and teacher of dance Barbara helps her students, "Understand the character of the dance, often a hurdle for the students." But she says that, "Once you've learned it, it's yours, internalized, you never forget it. There's a wonderful physical, spiritual and mental package you get when you dance."

You'd think this accomplished woman would sit back and rest on her well-deserved laurels, but not Barbara. Currently she's busy with inner-city social work tutoring 3rd, 4th and 5th graders in Merengue, and also coaching their crumping moves! She is also a Theology student with a goal to forming a liturgical dance company to combine her spiritual love and her love of dance.

Nearly everyone that I interviewed for this book, especially the instructors, had a 'Barbara story.' She is a remarkable woman who has touched lives through the power of her dance.

Barbara and Tim Haller's Bio

Barbara and Tim Haller are four-time United States Professional Theatrical Arts Champions. By winning this National Championship Ballroom Dancing Title for the fourth time in 1999, the Hallers made ballroom competition history by becoming only the second theatrical arts dance team to win the title four times since the inception of the United States Ballroom Championships in 1971.

Theatrical Arts is one of the most physically demanding styles of dance. Unlike the other competitive ballroom dance styles, it borrows significantly from gymnastics and ballet. Typically danced with one team on the floor at a time, the Cabaret style routines of Theatrical Arts are filled with complicated lifts, drops, splits and other risk figures. Theatrical Arts most closely resembles pairs figure skating — beautiful, exciting and graceful.

The Hallers were recent recipients of the Feather Award, ballroom dancing's equivalent of the movie industry's Oscar. Barbara and Tim also received the Feather Award's highest honor, the Publication Award, recognizing them as the "most accomplished Theatrical Arts dancers" in the United States. Other notable past recipients of the Publication Award include Cyd Charisse, Juliet Prowse and Donald O'Connor (Singin' in the Rain).

Frequent performers with the Cincinnati Pops Orchestra, the Hallers have been seen in the Pops' *Symphantasy VII An American in Paris,* the televised PBS holiday special *New Year's Eve Big Band Hit Parade, A Grand Viennese Ball*, and *Gotta Dance*. The Hallers have also performed with the Naples Philharmonic, Illinois Philharmonic, Middletown Symphony and the Carmon DeLeone Orchestra. Barbara and Tim also performed with the Cincinnati Symphony Orchestra for the first time in a special New Year's Eve concert, *A French Affair to Remember.* The Hallers owned and operated the Arthur Murray Dance Studios of Dayton, Ohio from 1984 to 2004.

Barbara and Tim Haller have been featured soloists on PBS's popular and nationally televised program, *Championship Ballroom Dancing* for an unprecedented nine years, including PBS's 20th Anniversary television special *Legends of Dance*.

Svetlana Hollenbaugh

Svetlana is the total dance package. If she were a football player she'd be one of those triple threats, someone who can run, pass and play defense. With 30 years of experience in a variety of dance disciplines she embraces ballet, ballroom, folk and ethnic styles. When you hit the floor with Svetlana you better have your dance game ON! Before doing this book and interviewing her I'd danced with her, at the studio and in social settings. After hearing her incredible history I'm proud to have danced with her, and a little intimidated by the experience. Luckily, she's as charming as she is talented.

As a young girl in the Mari El republic of the Soviet Union Svetlana was entranced by the dancers she saw on television. Like children worldwide she bounced and gyrated, trying to imitate the images on the flickering screen before her.

There has always been a dance tradition in Europe and the Soviet Union; young people took dance classes as part of the standard educational curriculum. Often the gifted students were fast-tracked into programs to take advantage of their inherent talents. Svetlana wanted to dance better...and she had talent.

She attended a Fine Arts school, learning different styles of dance: ballet, folk, and ballroom. Her curriculum also included theater arts, language and music, the accordion! She received a Ballet Master Degree and worked a s a teacher.

According to Svetlana, "Most girls try to dance to look beautiful, it's exciting, and everybody wants to be on the stage." That was her destiny; she became an integral part of the Mari El dance company. It was, according to Svetlana, "A big family of sixty dancers." As a member of this professional dance troupe she toured the Soviet Union, from the Ukraine to Vladivostok. She performed throughout Europe and Asia, dancing before dignitaries and royalty in Poland, East Germany, Spain, Belgium, Portugal, Finland, Hungary, Cambodia, India, and Sri Lanka.

In each place they visited, the group incorporated many of the dances of that region. This provided Svetlana with a wealth of ethnic dance exper- ience.

Eventually she found her way to the United States, and an interview at the local Arthur Murray dance studio. In addition to teaching at the dance studio she's also conducted seminars on regional, folk and ethnic dances at local ballet schools.

Svetlana believes that dancing is good exercise, "Very healthy, you're always moving, always working."

Naturally, someone with her extensive professional background appreciates the performance aspects of dance. Svetlana likes the expressive and theatrical attributes of dance, saying that in dance, "You want to show the lady how beautiful she is."

Her favorite style of dance, of the many diverse styles she has mastered, is the ethnic, folkloric dance. But in ballroom, she prefers the Latin dances to the smoother styles. According to Svetlana, on the Latin dances you can, "Use all of your body, and express yourself."

She enjoys teaching dance and working with people to help them reach their potential, and it always makes her feel good to see her students walk out of the dance studio with a smile on their face.

Terry Irwin

Terry Irwin is a frequent visitor to the Dayton Arthur Murray dance studio, directing and choreographing shows for the Dayton studio for the last eight years. As a nationally known dance coach and choreographer he works with students and professionals alike, refining their technique and choreographing stage performances and show routines.

He is the president of TC Dance Club International, a former Pro Am Champion of American Smooth, American Rhythm and Theatrical Arts styles, and a National Dance Council of America (NDCA) Certified Adjudicator.

Some of his more distinguished credits include: Choreographer and Principal Director for Bob Hope's US Tour, Choreographer and Principal Director for Miss America Pageants, and Choreographer and Principal Director for Frankie Vali & The Four Seasons

Terry has choreographed community theatrical productions of Peter Pan, Joseph and the Amazing Technicolor Dreamcoat, The Little Shop of Horrors, West Side Story, Wizard of Oz, Godspell, and Glory of the Morning.

Paula Kirkland

I'd seen Paula at the dance studio from time to time, although her more regular venue was the studio across town. She'd usually show up on the party nights when the two studios got together to dance. Her dancing had an elegant, almost ethereal quality to it, and watching her effortless moves and graceful extensions always put me in mind of ice skating legend Peggy Fleming. So it was a treat when we showed up at the studio one night to find she was to be our instructor for the evening.

When her mother took her older brother to tumbling classes, three-year old Paula saw other young girls in leotards moving about and wanted to join. It wasn't 'dance' so much as it was, "Creative movement," according to Paula, but it lit a fire in her nonetheless, and she found herself enrolled in a local dance school.

In high school she was still dancing and on the drill team. As a teenager, Paula participated in an exchange student program that gave her the opportunity to travel and dance in St. Petersburg and Moscow, Russia. But as graduation came nearer she realized that she wanted to continue. Her next stop was the Dayton Ballet School where she found herself behind, and worked feverishly to close the gaps in her technical and performance skills.

While attending Wright State University she joined the Dayton Contemporary Dance Company II, a pre-professional dance troupe where she entered in total dance immersion. She studied ballet every day, along with courses in modern and jazz dance, and danced at night, calling it, "The best training I had."

Earning a Bachelor of Fine Arts in Dance she decided she wanted to try ballroom dancing. Barbara and Time Haller were national dance sensations, and Paula had followed their exploits on television and in the papers. She started as a student in December 1998 and was teaching ballroom dancing in March of 1999. Although Paula admitted she, "Never thought I'd want to teach," after starting she, "really enjoyed it." Personally she views it as a game in which she tries to, "Help someone learn what's right for them." She strives to be a positive influence and, "Help people improve themselves and work towards their goals and dreams."

As to the benefits of dance, for Paula it's a personal thing, "Benefits are individual; everyone is searching to improve themselves, and we all find fulfillment in different things. For me it's been a way of life." When she was younger it was "Something I wanted, worked hard for, doing what I wanted to do...the discipline." But now she finds she enjoys, "The movement and expression."

For Paula, all dances are special, but forced to pick a favorite she likes the American Smooth, a favorite being the Waltz.

She and Mario competed as a couple, dancing in competitions across the country in New York, Florida, Tennessee, and Ohio. In 2003 they were named the Arthur Murray Rising Star Smooth Champions. Paula has worked with children and given dance exhibitions at schools, churches, festivals, cancer treatment centers, and even correctional institutes.

Paula describes dancing as, "Movement to music, a visual expression of what you hear. I hear beautiful music and it makes me want to dance." For those who witness a performance by her, it may be that we hear beautiful music and think of Paula.

Mario Kraszewski

Mario is pure energy and enthusiasm. Some people dance erotically; some make it dangerous and powerful. Mario makes it fun. His dancing is infused with life; it's an electric, high-energy performance that commands attention.

Watching him perform and instruct only reinforces my impressions. So it came as no surprise when he told me how he came to dance.

It seems that there was this group of pretty young girls...

Mario's story begins many years ago near Warsaw, Poland. As a young 10-year old he was making his way to a religious training class at his church. As he walked across town he passed in front of the city's cultural center where he saw a group of young girls. Wondering what these girls could be doing, and wanting to get to know them better, he crossed the street. These lovely girls were on a break from their dance class, and when the break was over, young Mario followed them upstairs to find ballroom dance lessons in progress. The following week he became a student, unaware that he was destined to dance and become a successful competitor and studio owner.

From that dance class of two hundred students, Mario was one of only twenty selected for competition. Paired with a skilled partner, they danced together for the next nine years.

Mario was also a professional soccer player. After three years he left soccer for the world of dance. Dance provided the same competitive aspects he found in soccer, but he really liked traveling around Europe, dressing up, and being in the glamorous environment of European competitive dance. The social aspects of dance have always been an important part of Mario's life.

When he arrived in America he taught ballroom dancing in New York City. In 1998 he came to Dayton, Ohio with a world of dance experience and only a rudimentary command of English. Walking through those studio doors he told his dance partner, "Someday I will own this studio." In 2002 he bought his first dance studio and in 2004 he purchased the second.

Mario believes that there are many benefits to be derived from ballroom dance. "People who want to learn to dance don't realize that ballroom dancing will change their lives forever." It's not just, "Learning the steps," but that their perspective on, "social life will change completely." He considers dance lessons at an Arthur Murray studio to be a, "...social life education college."

Self expression, according to Mario, is another of the many benefits of ballroom dancing. Ballroom dance can be the, "Source where people can achieve their childhood dreams, dressing up and being on stage...dreams lost in life can be realized...a fairy tale chance to do what they want to do."

From the teacher's perspective Mario loves to help people every day. He says that sometimes he, "Leaves the memory, they don't realize it now, but in a year they may realize that, 'Mario changed my life.'" This missionary aspect of dance, the literal changing of lives, is one that Mario feels is most important.

When asked what attracted him to teaching Mario explained, "If you're a dancer the teaching is 'given,' it goes hand-in-hand with being a dancer." In his opinion there are two kinds of dance teachers. One: the great technician, who teaches the way they know best, not always the most effective. Two: the very trained, they realize what is important for the student at that point in time. Mario and his staff seem to fit into the latter category, working with each student's strengths and weaknesses to provide the right level of instruction at the right time.

In America, Mario found that, "America is unique

about the social aspect of dance; it doesn't exist anywhere else in the world. Why? Americans are very outgoing people. The dance studio is a place to get together, where it is safe, and people can share similar interests. At the studio we can share one another's passion."

In addition to being something of a social philosopher, Mario's sense of community is strong. One of his biggest personal accomplishments was being the first to establish a wheel chair dance federation in Poland. In 1996, he and his partner, who was wheelchair bound, won the World Cup Championship in Holland. This wheelchair federation gave the participants a chance to do something that, "Others take for granted...gives them a shot at being in a pretty world." Continuing to bring the world of dance to others, Mario works with local schools in Dayton, Ohio to conduct ballroom dance classes for their students.

Mario won several championships in Poland and was the Arthur Murray Rising Star Champion in 2003.

When asked about his favorite style of dance Mario replied, "The Paso Doble." Then he thought for a minute and said, "It depends on the partner. I am a giver, and dance to the level of the partner I am with, trying to make this person as happy as possible."

Justyna Masajlo

When Radoslaw 'Radek' Rogowski and Justyna Masajlo take the floor it's theirs; they own it, they control every square inch of it! I've watched this dynamic pair perform exhibitions, and they literally danced to every corner. Whether it's a smooth Waltz or a hot and frenzied Latin number, when these two dance every eye is on them.

Justyna's body moves with a snake-like fluidity, then she stops and turns with such quick timing you'd think she was a high-performance machine. This rapid-fire mix of sharp precision and seductive undulations is mesmerizing.

A thirteen year dance veteran, Justyna has been dancing with Radek for the last five years. As is common among most European-trained dancers Justyna began in the typical school dance class. A dance instructor came to one of her school meetings and her mother asked if she wanted to try dance lessons. After a year of lessons the process of natural selection reduced the dance pool from thirty couples to only five, and Justyna's talent insured she survived the cut. She was inspired by her Polish coach, a very accomplished dancer, who performed in the United States on Broadway. She plunged into dance, learning the ten international ballroom dances.

During her competitive days in Europe Justyna danced in over 250 competitions across the continent, touring Poland, Russia, Germany and Latvia. Since coming to America she and Radek have begun to test the competitive waters of America.

What attracted Justyna to teaching dance was, "Helping people, if I know how to dance I can help people through my dance." Besides working with adults she's extended her talents to six and seven year-olds, grooming another generation of dancers.

Justyna says that one of the benefits of dancing is, "For the woman is good exercise, makes you feel young," and that when dancing women can, "Be beautiful, be something or someone different."

Justyna's favorites are the Latin dances. "Woman can show her inside, how woman can be sexy."

I don't doubt that one bit.

Radoslaw "Radek" Rogowski

While Radek possesses all the technical skills of the professional dancer his art exudes something more...danger and mystery. He seems to be that 'bad boy' on the floor, the rogue that women find irresistible.

Not surprisingly, given the ubiquitous nature of dance in European culture, Radek was first exposed to dance by his family. In Radek's world everyone danced. He explained that in America a wedding might last from 6:00 p.m. to 10:00 p.m., while in Poland the wedding would go from 6:00 p.m. to 6:00 a.m. the next morning, with continual dancing the entire time! His mother took him to a dance class, and for the first five years Radek was not enthused about dance and didn't take it seriously. He had fun dancing, enjoyed the social aspects, but had no interest in competing.

This began to change as Radek saw what the world of dance had to offer. "In Poland, dancing gave you a different life...different world between the street and dance...dance was like a big family." The social skills gleaned from dancing were also a plus. "I learned how to talk with women."

Entering the European competitive dance community Radek competed in over 150 competitions in Europe. He has now been dancing for eleven years.

When asked about the benefits, Radek agreed with most of his teaching peers that it was, "Great exercise." He says that listening to the music, "Starts my heart beating."

Radek is adept at all styles of ballroom dance. He has that consummate skill that makes it look easy enough that we might all think we could do it.

He remains involved in dance and teaching people by the very nature of the personal contact involved. He likes to, "Meet different kinds of people, what they look like, how they feel." Competing in, and teaching dance, has allowed Radek to, "Meet how many different kinds of people there are in the world," and get to know their, "Likes and dislikes."

Natasha Yushanov

Natasha had two dreams, to write and to dance. Seeing as she has now collaborated on a book that contains some of her dancing exploits I'd say she's been somewhat successful in realizing her dreams.

Natasha is an original, one-of-a-kind. But that's too vague, not really a good description. She's not a Diva, but she commands center stage. She's not a Prima Donna, but she can get her own way. Ordinary English words don't fit this exceptional woman so I will look abroad. Let's call her...Maitresse. I prefer the French term, Maitresse, over the German, Lehrerin, or the Russian, Pyccku. Maitresse means 'A woman who is a teacher.' That fits Natasha, a teacher, a passionate and driven teacher, but a teacher.

When Natasha was four years old her father took the family to visit relatives who possessed a wondrous machine, the television. Young Natasha looked at the ballet unfolding on this magic box and knew she wanted to dance. She started dancing ballet at the age of six and danced for six years before trying her hand at the ballroom style. She was too tall to successfully pair up with any available partner. Her only real ballroom memory from that time was her instructor telling her, "Natasha, you're doing a very good hip motion on the Cha-Cha." She drifted away from dance, but the longing never abated.

In 1995 she found herself in Akron, Ohio, cleaning houses. At the house of one well-to-do client, an older woman, she noticed a picture of the woman. Her employer was clad in a beautiful ballroom gown and dancing with a younger male partner. Natasha asked about the picture. The woman explained that ballroom dancing was something she always wanted to do, and now that she was older, with the time and the means, she was indulging in her love of dance. Natasha kept that image in her mind, wondering when it would be her time.

Events later found her in Dayton Ohio. When friends decided to take dance lessons Natasha was invited along to partner with one of the men. He wasn't the best of partners, but she was dancing. Her partner purchased a 10-lesson package but moved away before the lessons were complete, leaving Natasha with the remaining lessons.

The final two lessons found her in the arms of very accomplished dance instructors and she was swept away. Unfortunately, just as she was beginning to feel the passion of dance, the private lessons were over.

One afternoon, as she was leaving the studio, one of the dance instructors said, "Why don't you apply for a job?"

Natasha glumly thought, *A job? I don't want to clean the studio.*

Obviously seeing the look on her face the instructor continued, "As a dance instructor, a job as a dance instructor. You can teach people to dance, they'll train you."

Natasha went home to consider the possibility. She had many anxious moments trying to work up the courage to come in and ask for a job as a dance instructor. She said she didn't know, "How I gathered the guts," but she called the studio owner, Barbara Haller, and asked to come in and speak to her.

At the meeting Barbara told Natasha that she didn't have any private lessons left, but that she did have some group lessons and party nights left. There followed a silent pause and Natasha replied, "Yes, but I came to ask for a job as a dance instructor."

Barbara thought for a moment, finally saying, "Well, with your ballet background, I don't see why not."

Now those of us today who know Natasha as the

domineering Dance Mistress who rules the floor, will undoubtedly have trouble imagining her as a shy, reluctant job applicant. Again, that's perhaps another example of how dance can change people's lives, allowing people to become and achieve, realize their full potential.

So Natasha embarked on a career as a dance teacher. In March 1998 she started as a dance student, in August she started training as a dance instructor and in September she taught her first student. Barbara told Natasha that she was going to, "Make you into a star. You are going to be my counselor." To which Natasha asked, "What is counselor?"

She is now the studio manager, realizing her dream to dance and succeeding at it; from cleaning houses in Akron and gazing longingly at pictures on the wall, to managing a dance studio.

On the benefits of dance, Natasha says it, "Helps people to see who they are. In dancing there is a niche for everyone to fulfill their dreams through dance. Dance gives you the ground, it shapes people, both physically, and where they are and where they need to go. It is one of the most accessible forms of art, having social and public purposes and applications."

What does she like best about dancing? For

Natasha it's the self-expression, that perfect moment when, "The music, the partner and the moods all match."

She has no favorite style of dance, "I don't care, as long as it's passionate." That's a fact. I've watched Natasha dance and I've danced with her. She brings passion and theatricality to her dance. But even she admits to only recently, after twelve to thirteen 'shows,' being able to find the freedom to really perform and enjoy it. In dance, even for a professional, there is always more to learn, more to do.

She was naturally attracted to teaching. Her mother was a teacher, and when the teachers met at the house for coffee or a social visit it usually turned into an ad hoc teacher's conference. By the third grade Natasha was assisting the teachers in her school. Becoming a dance instructor was an easy fit for her. A visiting pro at the studio once observed her, barely out of training, giving a lesson and asked Barbara where Natasha's, "Natural teacher's demeanor came from."

For Natasha teaching is all about sharing, "When I can communicate, and the student makes it part of their experience, we share the excitement." Natasha, the teacher, the Maitresse.

Supporting Cast

Listed Alphabetically

The more I worked on this book, and talked to other students at the studio, the more I came to see the ability dance has to impact people's lives. I asked them why they danced and what it gave back to them. These are their stories.

Doug: Computer Engineer

"It gave me my life back."

Doug is a single parent, something that many can identify with. One day his young son confronted him: "Dad, you need to get out and do something, you're boring, and you stay at home all the time." On reflection Doug had to agree with this off-the-cuff, juvenile assessment. He was boring; he'd drifted apart from his former close-knit group of friends, but...what to do about it?

In the movie *Zorro*, Anthony Hopkins tells the young

Zorro-wanna-be Antonio Banderas, "When the student is ready, the master will appear." And so it was with Doug. The boring, stay-at-home Doug opened his mail box to find a direct mail advertisement from the local Dayton Arthur Murray Dance Studio. He called the studio to inquire about the two free dance lessons advertised on the flyer. They asked if he could be there in thirty minutes.

Three years later Doug is still dancing and appearing in many of the shows and productions. He says dance gave him the ability to take up something new, and have a vision of the things he could accomplish, "People react and communicate differently with me now, I seem to have more confidence."

"It gave me my life back, it came at the perfect moment in my life and made my life more fulfilling." Originally he saw a gloomy transition from youth to old age, with no concept of anything else, "Like I had to be old and dancing proved to me that I didn't have to be old."

Ervin: Contractor and Janice: Retired

"Dancing never gets old, there is always a challenge."

Janice began her dance lessons in February 2005. She'd retired from a career of teaching software programs and was looking for a new "life challenge," something to keep her mind and body active. She'd always harbored the desire to get on the dance floor and was tired of being a wallflower at weddings and parties. A friend told her that he and his wife were taking dance lessons and it seemed the ideal solution. When she told Ervin he replied, "You can take lessons, but I 'm not!"

Hoping to goad Ervin into the dance lessons she told him that it would mean she would be, "Dancing with other men." His reply: "That's all right." Fueled by the desire to learn to dance Janice started her lessons.

Six months later Ervin started attending the group lessons at the Friday night studio parties, and eighteen months later, he began his own private lessons.

Both enjoy the sense of accomplishment dancing provides, saying "Dancing never gets old; there's always a challenge to improve." No longer confined to the house on Friday and Saturday evenings, Ervin and Janice go out to clubs, entertain others with their dance routines, socialize, have fun and meet new friends. "We learned to dance ballroom to country music! It's so rewarding when people come up to us at the end of the evening, complimenting us on our dancing and telling us how much they enjoyed watching us."

According to Janice, "My confidence has greatly improved. I'm no longer shy...I love the freedom of expression that dance has given me."

Judy: Dance Studio Administrative Assistant

"I started to live when I started to dance."

Judy is the Administrative Assistant/Bookkeeper at the local Arthur Murray studio. That innocuous job title covers a lot of ground and Judy touches the lives of everyone that ventures in and out of the studio, whether they realize it or not.

As you might expect Judy is a dancer herself, having been involved with ballroom dancing since 1977. After dancing at her cousin's wedding, she found herself in pain. Reasoning that dancing shouldn't be a painful experience she decided to fix the problem with formal dance lessons. And so began a journey into the world of dance that continues 29 years later.

Even after all those years the joy of dancing hasn't diminished. She loves doing show pieces saying she was, "Always smiling when I danced."

Besides giving her more confidence dancing landed her both a career and a husband. She met her husband, a dance instructor, at the studio. She'd been a dance student for five years when studio owner Barbara Haller offered her a job as a receptionist, beginning her career in the dance industry.

Among her many responsibilities are bookkeeping, student accounts, lesson payments, reports, and special events. She organizes the twice-yearly Dayton Dance Classic. In the past, at other studios, she's even been called upon to step in and give a lesson when an instructor found themselves double-booked.

It's not simply her job as an Administrative Assistant and Bookkeeper that Judy enjoys, but the chance to witness, every day, how dance changes people's lives. She gets to, "See people improve...to know we are giving people benefits to life."

As for herself she says, "I started to live when I started to dance."

Gloria: Sales

"It has given me more confidence."

As a girl Gloria loved to dance, attending all the dances when she was in high school. But, as with most of us, life happens and we embark on careers. Still, the urge to dance never left her; she wanted to expand her knowledge of the art, which eventually led her to Arthur Murray.

Gloria has been dancing at the studio for three years, finding many of the same benefits from dance that others enjoy. She's increased her flexibility, her balance and even lost weight.

For Gloria, dance, "Has given me more confidence, especially being in front of people," a definite asset in the sales world.

Joe: Chemical Engineer

"Dance has become a part of me."

When I asked Joe how long he'd been dancing he said, "Since June 7th 2005." When a person can tell me 'exactly' when they started dancing it makes me believe that they are either obsessive compulsive types, or that dance has truly impacted their lives. I was surprised at Joe's answer not only for the exactness of the date, but because he is a very good dancer, much better than I would have imagined for someone who'd trained only a few months.

Following the tragic death of his wife, Joe's life became one of work and little else. In his own words he was, "Functioning, but wasn't living, leading a drab existence with no social life." One of his friends suggested he try dancing as a way to get out, meet people and make the social contacts to get his life back.

Joe ended up with Natasha as his teacher, saying she, "Was very good for me." Natasha had a compassionate understanding of where Joe was and helped him, "Get into the music and the rhythm." Joe, "Found it therapeutic."

What is it that Joe gets from dance? For him it's the intimate connection between dance and emotion. According to Joe it, "Brings joy to me to be able to get on the floor and dance...bring my own expression into it. I started living again once I started to dance. Dance has become a part of me."

Joe: University Professor and Jean: Housewife

"Dancing is something we can enjoy together"

Joe and Jean have been dancing a little over five years. It began for them one evening when they happened to watch another couple dance and were impressed by the technique they witnessed. At that point they thought it would be, "Fun to learn that skill."

Again, dance fate intervened as Joe and Jean were contacted by the new Arthur Murray dance studio in their area.

For them dancing is, "Something we can enjoy together; it's the exercise, social aspects and the challenge of moving in unison with the music," that keeps them coming back for more.

Linda: Accountant and Holistic Health Practitioner

*"This is the first creative thing
I have been good at."*

Linda's journey into the world of dance began in 1999 when she was invited to the Dayton Opera Ball by a man who said he was a "Fabulous dancer." Linda admits she was "Not, so I called Arthur Murray." She always wanted to dance but never knew how, nor had the opportunity.

For Linda it opened, "A side of me I had not known was there." She loves learning and loves the challenge of dance, saying it is, "Great exercise." Linda admits that when she first came to the studio she was, "Unsure of myself and more shy than I am now."

But dancing allowed this formerly shy accountant to blossom. She admits that the parties are great fun and a safe place for single women. Dancing, for her, "Is the first creative thing I have been good at."

Lynne: Mental Health Therapist

*"I'm probably in the best shape
I have ever been in my life."*

Although she said she'd only been ballroom dancing for seven months Lynne looks great on the floor, tall, lean and graceful. She enjoyed three years of country-western dancing in the 90's, but drifted away from dance for almost ten years. And that was unusual, because Lynne loves to dance. She even met her husband, 14 years ago, while dancing.

But she missed dance and decided to come back, this time ballroom style. What brought her back was an interest in doing some Pro / Am competitions. She also wanted to dance again for the exercise.

When asked what she got from dance she said it was, "The challenge of learning the steps and technique." And like most people, she simply enjoys the sheer fun of being on the floor.

Has dancing changed her life? According to Lynne, "Absolutely! I've met some great people and I'm probably in the best shape I have ever been in my life. I love being out on the floor having fun and enjoying the dance."

Marcia: Dance Studio Receptionist

*"I didn't think anything could
be so much fun."*

At a 1997 Christmas party, Marcia received a gift certificate for complimentary dance lessons, thus beginning her foray into what would become a life of dance. Although trained as a Registered Nurse Marcia found her calling when the dance studio expanded its support staff and offered her a job as the receptionist. She schedules lessons, answers the phone, greets students and provides a warm welcome for all who enter the studio.

Since entering the world of dance, Marcia says her Friday nights have changed. What used to be clipping a coupon for a burger and maybe popcorn and a movie for she and her husband has now become a weekly evening of dance.

Marcia loves the music, learning the technical aspects of dance, and participating in shows and competitions. According to her she is, "Living in the fun lane, I didn't think anything could be so much fun!" In addition to developing her own dance craft, Marcia enjoys seeing other people learn dance skills.

As the Dayton Arthur Murray Dance Studio receptionist, Marcia is usually the first person people meet when they walk in the studio. Being a dance student herself Marcia, "Knows how people feel when they walk in the door the first time." She loves the positive atmosphere that permeates the studio and looks at each person that walks in the door as a, "Ray of sunshine." As that first 'face' to the customer she welcomes them as part of the studio family.

To quote Natasha, "I've heard many people referring to her as 'our angel'."

Stefanie: Equal Employment Opportunity Counselor

"Dancing gave me the strength to make the changes that gave me my life back."

Stefanie has been dancing since July 2004, drawn to the art because she wanted to learn to dance in order to attend a 'Big Band' theme birthday party. While she was surprised at the technical and challenging nature of dance she admitted it's the, "Toughest job I'll ever love."

When asked if dancing had changed her life she responded with a resounding, "Oh yes!" Following the dissolution of her marriage Stefanie was "...shocked at how socially inept I had become." She didn't know, "...how to be comfortable in a group, I'd lost all my self confidence, my ability to function and be comfortable in social settings."

"Dancing gave me the strength to make the changes that gave me my life back. If it had not been for the studio with all its activities, I'm not sure how I would have made the transition back to the real world. I slowly learned how to be a real person again."

"Love the floor, love the woman, love yourself."

Natasha

About the Author

Greg Causey is an author, management consultant, blues guitarist, drummer - and dance student. He lives in Ohio with his wife Joan. Other books by Gregory (Greg) Causey may be found at Amazon.com and Barnes & Nobles.com.

The author can be contacted at his web sites:
www.dancingwithnatasha.com

www.insaneworkshops.com